Notes from the

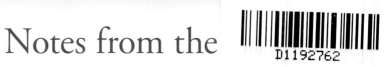

Welcome to a glimpse into the world of international handwork. At Stitch Publications our wish is for you to be able to explore beyond the boundaries of the country you live in to experience and see what other fiber artists are doing.

In many countries, rather than learning from various books, quilters and crafters study under a single master, spending years progressing from simple techniques to the extremely difficult. Intricate designs are celebrated, and sewing, embroidery, and quilting by hand is honored, and as such, appliqué, embroidery, and quilting by hand is the typical method used to quilt.

This book was written in its original language, Japanese, by celebrated artist Reiko Mori. We have done our best to make the directions for each embroidery project easy to understand and fairly simple to figure out if you have some level of sewing or crafting experience, while maintaining the appearance and intent of the original author and publisher.

We hope the beautiful and unique handmade embroidered items in this book inspire and encourage you to make them for yourself.

- Important Tips Before You Begin -

The embroidery designs and patterns are relatively simple and self-explanatory. Both beginners and those who are most advanced in embroidery skills should not have a problem doing the embroidery. When it comes to the sewing and crafting of the projects, such as the mini boxes and bags, etc., the following facts might suggest that intermediate or advanced crafters will be more comfortable working on these projects.

- Techniques -

The techniques and stitches used for the embroidery projects are detailed on pages 39–43, with additional stitches interspersed throughout the instructional pages. Ms. Mori has designed the embroidery patterns to be used as you like or as part of crafted objects, which are somewhat more challenging. The patterns and project instructions are located on pages 44–79. She assumes that the creator is familiar with sewing, crafting, and bag-making techniques to some degree and thus relies heavily on the creator's ability to figure out the directions that are not specifically written out. It is advisable to read through and understand each project's instructions from beginning to end.

- Measurements -

The original designs were created using the metric system for dimensions. In order to assist you, we have included the imperial-system measurements in brackets. However, please note that the samples that appear in the book were created and tested using the metric system. Thus, you will find that if you use the imperial measurements to make the projects, the items you make will not be exactly the same size as when using the metric measurements.

- Patterns/Templates -

Full pattern information for the embroidery designs are included in the instructions for each project, on pages 44–79. One must read through all the instructions, illustrations, and captions carefully to understand what size to cut the fabric and related materials and how to handle seam allowances.

Stitch Publications, 2018

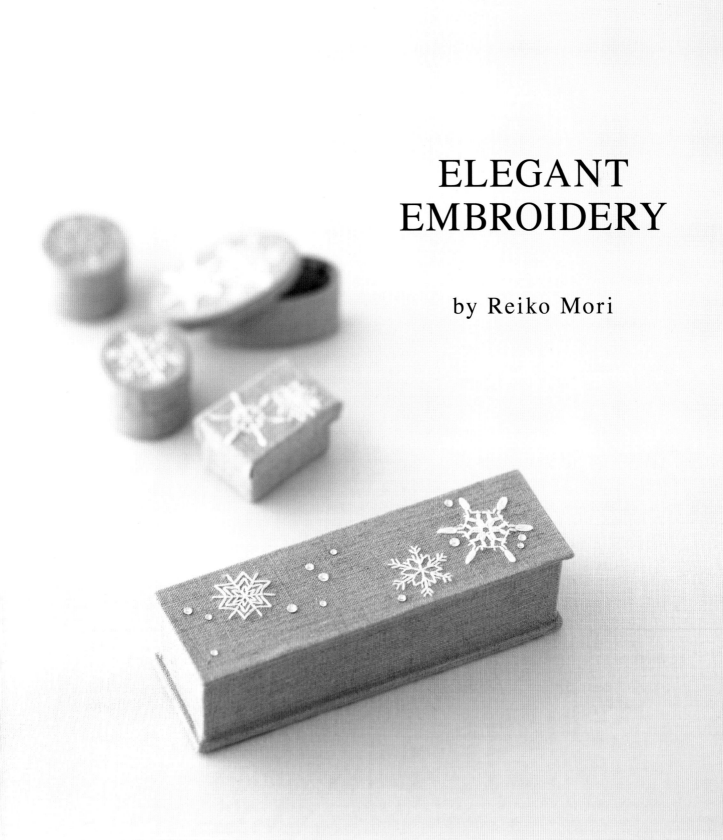

ELEGANT EMBROIDERY

by Reiko Mori

Contents

Stitchwork

4

◆ All embroidery floss (both standard and metallic) used in this book is manufactured by Olympus (No. 25).
◆ All embroidery stitches used are specified for each pattern.
◆ The floss colors shown may appear slightly different when seen in person.

Stitchwork 1

Black Collection

Little black dress

I imagine Grace Kelly might have worn this dress.

Instructions → page 44

Jewelry box

Instructions → page 45

Favorite things

I love to design small motifs of things I like.

Instructions → page 47

Petit boxes

The perfect size to store earrings, rings, or memories.

Instructions → page 64

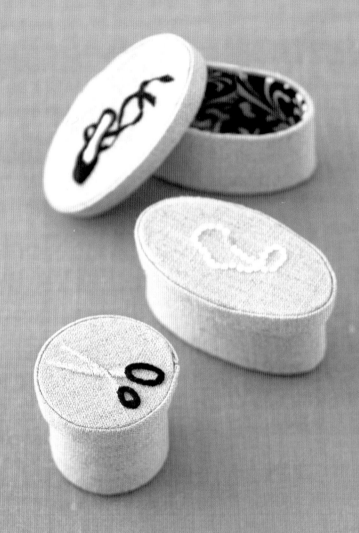

Lace lingerie

Who doesn't love to wear a little bit of mystery?

Instructions → page 48

Glasses case

Instructions → page 49

Stitchwork 2

Flower Collection

Violets

The shades of purple are captured beautifully in nature.
The posy reminds me of my youth.

Instructions → page 50

Tote bag 1

Instructions → page 62

Chamomile

The fragrance of chamomile gently drifts across a meadow.
Hardworking honeybees add charm to the tote bag.

Instructions → page 51

Tote bag 2

Instructions → page 62

Hollyhocks

Romantic and colorful hollyhocks are beautiful in any garden.
Add a watering can to make a larger pouch.

Instructions → page 52

Pouch

Instructions → page 57

Climbing roses

*My heart dances with delightful memories of seasons past
when the roses quietly begin to bloom in the spring.*

Instructions → page 54

Pocket board

A pocket board is a clever way to hold and display notes and cards.

Instructions → page 55

Stitchwork 3

Marine Collection

Summer vacation

Summer vacation is just around the corner. This year I dream of going to the Mediterranean.

Instructions → page 58

Pouches

Pouches with wide openings such as these are so easy to use. Embroider a favorite design on the front and add a cute zipper pull for fun.

Instructions → page 56

Summer vacation

Instructions → page 58

SAILOR

Sailor

Nothing wrong with embroidering a handsome sailor in uniform!

Instructions → page 59

Marine de France

The French sailor uniforms come with charming red pom-poms on their hats.

Instructions → page 60

Porter

Porters are happy to deal with anything... even a talkative mynah bird.

Instructions → page 61

Stitchwork 4

Christmas Season Collection

Skater girl

This year I'm determined to master the cross-step!

Instructions → page 63

Tote bag 3

Totes and bags with wide flat bottoms are perfect for carrying lunch boxes.

Instructions → page 62

Monogram petit boxes

You'll have to figure out early who these are for if you plan to make these little boxes as Christmas presents.

Instructions → page 65

Monogram box

Instructions → page 67

Christmas wreath

Once we've hung the wreath on the front door we can begin to decorate the Christmas tree!

Instructions → page 74

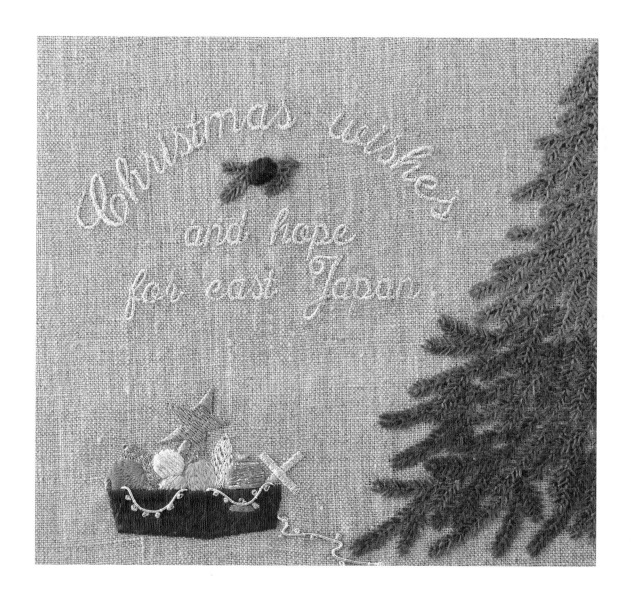

Christmas tree

Instructions → page 75

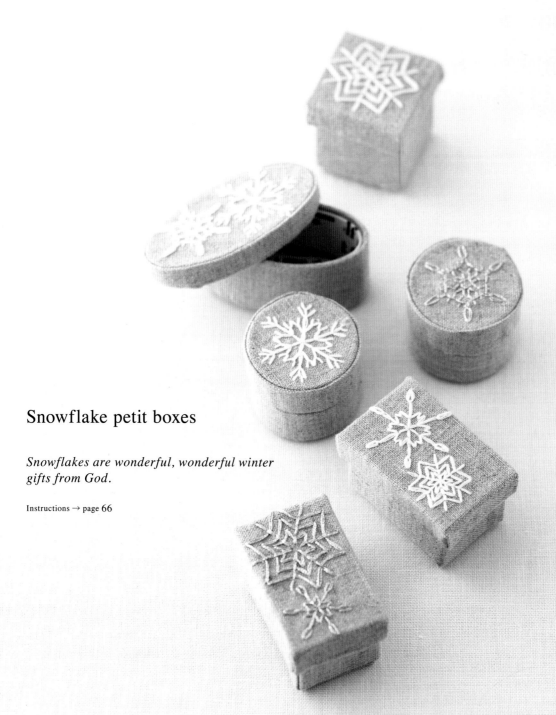

Snowflake petit boxes

Snowflakes are wonderful, wonderful winter gifts from God.

Instructions → page 66

Snowflake box

Instructions → page 67

Bundle Up

Bundle up in your winter finest to go out on the town on Christmas Eve!

Instructions → pages 76, 77

Sunglasses bag

I always seem to misplace my favorite sunglasses.
This is one pair that I will never lose.

Instructions → pages 78, 79

Chandelier bag

I can almost hear the theme song from "The Phantom of the Opera" when I see this chandelier on the side of the bag.

Instructions → pages 78, 79

Essential Notions & Tools

Thread

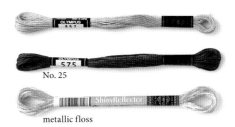

No. 25

metallic floss

The most popular and commonly used embroidery thread (or floss) is a six-strand No. 25 that comes in a loosely twisted hank. The floss can be separated into the required number of strands for each stitch or part of a design. The metallic floss (shown here is the Olympus Shiny Reflector Lamé) also is a six-strand floss. All the embroidery designs in this book use either the No. 25 or metallic floss. The design will specify the number of strands to use with each stitch.

Most, if not all, manufacturers of embroidery floss ship each hank with a paper sleeve around it, which denotes the specific color. Many have extremely slight color differences for use in shading, so it is critical to keep these sleeves with the floss as you stitch so you know which color to use for each section of the design.

Needles

No. 3

No. 5

No. 7

embroidery needles

Embroidery needles have larger eyes for easy threading and are pointed for smooth piercing. The lower the number, the thicker and longer the needle. Use a thicker needle when using thicker floss (or more strands); use a thinner needle when using thinner floss (or fewer strands.)

Scissors

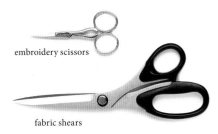

embroidery scissors

fabric shears

Small, sharp scissors are best when doing embroidery work. The finely pointed tips are necessary for snipping the floss or cutting away edges of appliqué seam allowances. Although not necessary, it is nice to have shears on hand for cutting the background fabric.

Fabric and Hoops

All the designs and projects in this book have been stitched and worked on linen. The natural linen gives the finished projects a sense of style and it looks more chic than plain cotton. Since linen tends to wrinkle, steam-iron your design lightly from the wrong side when it is complete. Whether or not you choose to use a hoop is up to you. I find that if I am using a slippery satin thread or have a lot of design area to embroider, it is advantageous to use a hoop.

Basic Techniques

Transferring the Pattern to the Fabric

1 Thoroughly iron the fabric to press out any wrinkles. Place the Chaco paper (tailor's tracing paper) right side down on the fabric, centered over where the design will go.

2 Place the design right side up, followed by a sheet of cellophane. The cellophane tends to be a bit slippery but protects the design from being punctured by the pen tip.

3 Use a ballpoint pen or stylus to firmly trace the design. Remove the paper design and cellophane when finished.

4 Use a marking pencil to go over and fill in any areas that were missed.

Preparing and Using Embroidery Floss

1 Holding the skein by the paper label, pull out the floss (note that all six strands are twisted into one) and cut the length you want to use.

2 Cut the floss to a length of about 40–50 cm [16"–20"].

3 Loosen the end of the floss and pull out one strand while lightly pinching the rest of the length.

4 Once you have pulled out the number of strands you need, match the ends of the strands together. Smooth the strands together. This should be done even if the instructions call for all six strands.

Threading the Embroidery Needle

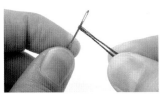

1 For easy threading, wrap the strands around the top of the needle and hold taut. Fold the floss in two.

2 Pinch the strands of floss while keeping them taut at the top of the needle (the side of eye); pull the floss off the top while it is still pinched between your fingertips.

3 Thread the flattened floss through the eye of the needle.

4 Leave about 10 cm [4"] of floss on one side of the threaded needle.

Anchoring the Ends of the Stitching

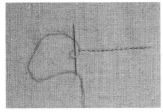

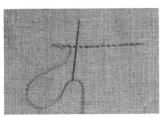

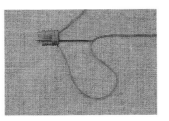

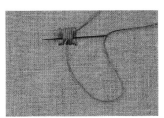

1 Rather than tying a knot, leave 3–4 cm [1¼"–1½"] of floss at the beginning on the wrong side.

2 Use your needle to thread the ends and weave through the first few stitches to secure; clip close to stitching.

3 In the case of the satin stitch, pass the ends over and under several of the vertical stitches.

4 Do this over several different sections to secure; clip close to the stitching.

39

Embroidery Stitches

* In order to show the step-by-step instructions clearly, I've used perle cotton (No. 5) in each of the following sections describing individual stitches.

Running Stitch

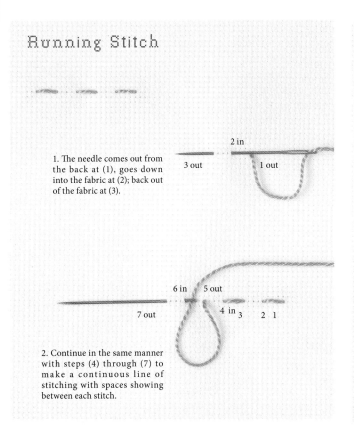

1. The needle comes out from the back at (1), goes down into the fabric at (2); back out of the fabric at (3).

2. Continue in the same manner with steps (4) through (7) to make a continuous line of stitching with spaces showing between each stitch.

Backstitch

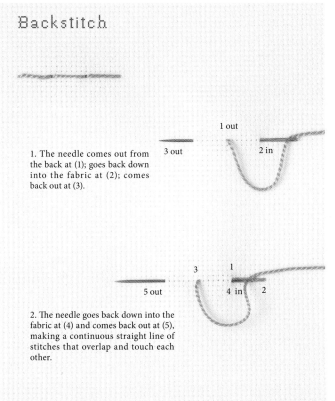

1. The needle comes out from the back at (1); goes back down into the fabric at (2); comes back out at (3).

2. The needle goes back down into the fabric at (4) and comes back out at (5), making a continuous straight line of stitches that overlap and touch each other.

Outline Stitch

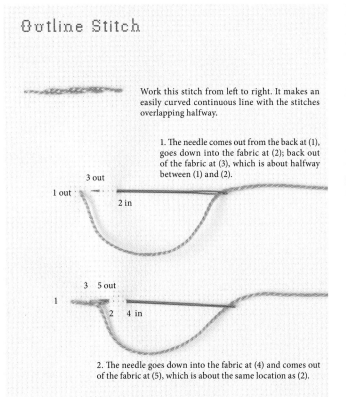

Work this stitch from left to right. It makes an easily curved continuous line with the stitches overlapping halfway.

1. The needle comes out from the back at (1), goes down into the fabric at (2); back out of the fabric at (3), which is about halfway between (1) and (2).

2. The needle goes down into the fabric at (4) and comes out of the fabric at (5), which is about the same location as (2).

Couching Stitch

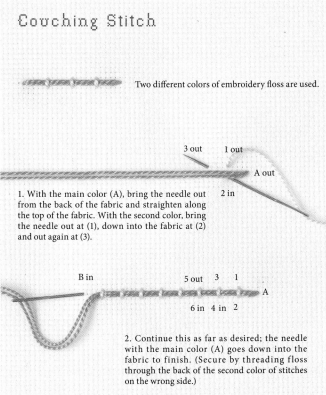

Two different colors of embroidery floss are used.

1. With the main color (A), bring the needle out from the back of the fabric and straighten along the top of the fabric. With the second color, bring the needle out at (1), down into the fabric at (2) and out again at (3).

2. Continue this as far as desired; the needle with the main color (A) goes down into the fabric to finish. (Secure by threading floss through the back of the second color of stitches on the wrong side.)

Chain Stitch

1. The needle comes out from the back at (1), goes down into the fabric at (2), which is the same location as (1); back out of the fabric at (3), pull the floss until there is an oval.

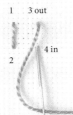

2. The needle goes down into the fabric at (4), which is the same place as (3) and comes out of the fabric at (5); pull the floss to create an oval of an identical size to the first one to start the chain.

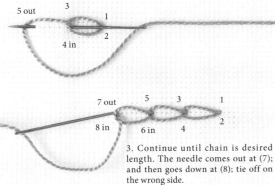

3. Continue until chain is desired length. The needle comes out at (7); and then goes down at (8); tie off on the wrong side.

Straight Stitch

1. The needle comes out from the back at (1), goes down into the fabric at (2); this creates a straight stitch.

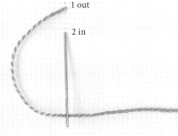

2. Bring the needle out again at (3), making sure it is even with the location of (1). The needle goes down at (4).

French Knot Stitch

Wrap the floss 2 times.

1. Bring the needle up through the background fabric at the position marked on the design. Lay it next to the floss. Press the needle down with the thumb and wrap the floss around the needle as many times as needed (two wraps are shown here).

2. Tug the floss to gather the wrapped floss down toward the head of the needle. Use your thumb to press down on top of the wraps so they won't loosen. Pull the needle all the way through while continuing to press firmly down on the wrapped floss to tighten and create a knot.

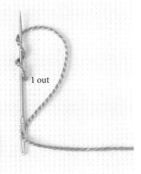

3. Push the tip of the needle down through the background fabric next to the knot. Tug on the floss to adjust the shape of the knot.

Wrap the floss 1 time.

4. To make a smaller knot, wrap your needle fewer times.

Lazy Daisy Stitch

1. The needle comes out from the back at (1), goes down into the fabric at (2), which is the same location as (1); bring the needle back out of the fabric at (3) with the tip on top of the floss; pull the floss until there is a looped oval.

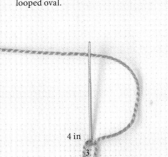

2. Go back down into the fabric at (4), which should be just on the other side of the floss loop to catch and hold it in place.

Embroidery Stitches

Fly Stitch

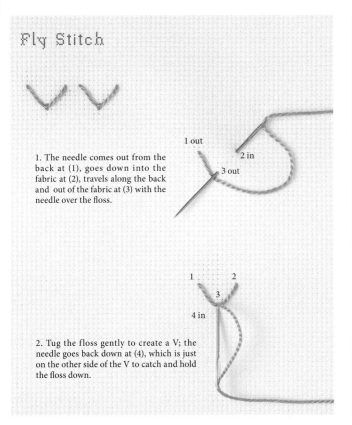

1. The needle comes out from the back at (1), goes down into the fabric at (2), travels along the back and out of the fabric at (3) with the needle over the floss.

2. Tug the floss gently to create a V; the needle goes back down at (4), which is just on the other side of the V to catch and hold the floss down.

Bullion Stitch

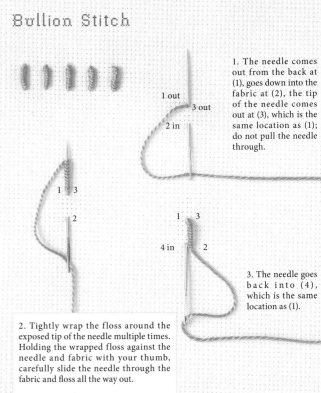

1. The needle comes out from the back at (1), goes down into the fabric at (2), the tip of the needle comes out at (3), which is the same location as (1); do not pull the needle through.

2. Tightly wrap the floss around the exposed tip of the needle multiple times. Holding the wrapped floss against the needle and fabric with your thumb, carefully slide the needle through the fabric and floss all the way out.

3. The needle goes back into (4), which is the same location as (1).

Overcast Stitch

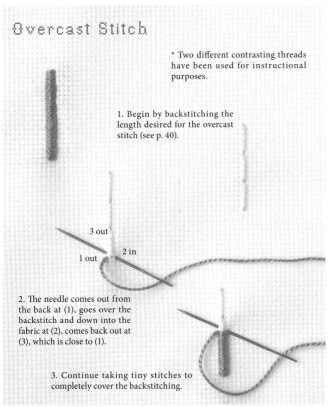

* Two different contrasting threads have been used for instructional purposes.

1. Begin by backstitching the length desired for the overcast stitch (see p. 40).

2. The needle comes out from the back at (1), goes over the backstitch and down into the fabric at (2), comes back out at (3), which is close to (1).

3. Continue taking tiny stitches to completely cover the backstitching.

Buttonhole Stitch

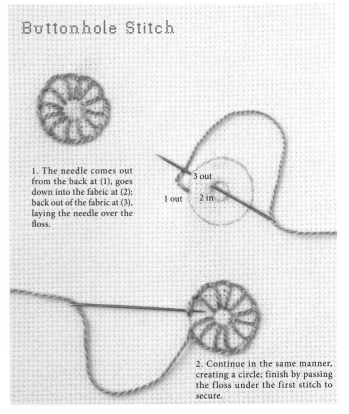

1. The needle comes out from the back at (1), goes down into the fabric at (2); back out of the fabric at (3), laying the needle over the floss.

2. Continue in the same manner, creating a circle; finish by passing the floss under the first stitch to secure.

Satin Stitch

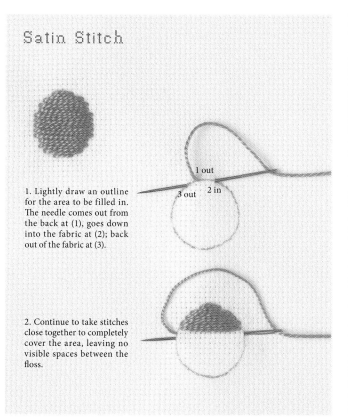

1. Lightly draw an outline for the area to be filled in. The needle comes out from the back at (1), goes down into the fabric at (2); back out of the fabric at (3).

1 out
3 out   2 in

2. Continue to take stitches close together to completely cover the area, leaving no visible spaces between the floss.

Double Satin Stitch

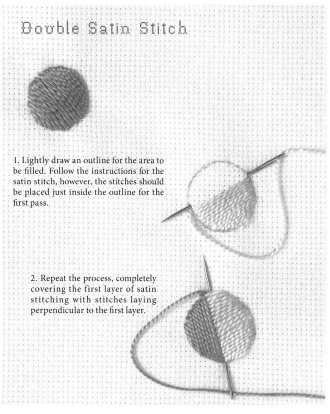

1. Lightly draw an outline for the area to be filled. Follow the instructions for the satin stitch, however, the stitches should be placed just inside the outline for the first pass.

2. Repeat the process, completely covering the first layer of satin stitching with stitches laying perpendicular to the first layer.

Long and Short Stitch

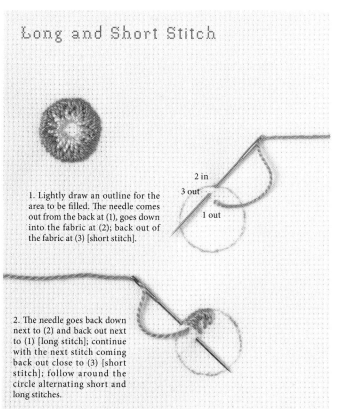

1. Lightly draw an outline for the area to be filled. The needle comes out from the back at (1), goes down into the fabric at (2); back out of the fabric at (3) [short stitch].

2 in
3 out
1 out

2. The needle goes back down next to (2) and back out next to (1) [long stitch]; continue with the next stitch coming back out close to (3) [short stitch]; follow around the circle alternating short and long stitches.

Turkey Work

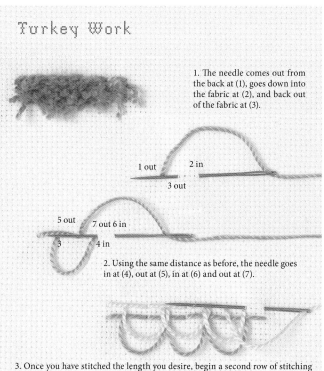

1. The needle comes out from the back at (1), goes down into the fabric at (2), and back out of the fabric at (3).

1 out   2 in
3 out

5 out   7 out 6 in
3   4 in

2. Using the same distance as before, the needle goes in at (4), out at (5), in at (6) and out at (7).

3. Once you have stitched the length you desire, begin a second row of stitching directly above the original row. Continue until you have all the rows required by the design. Cut the loops in the middle and trim the floss to the length desired.

Little black dress

shown on pages 4, 5

• Full-size embroidery patterns for the Little Black Dress stand-alone embroidery on p. 4 and and Jewelry Box on p. 5 are found below.
• The number in the parentheses stands for the number of strands used for the specific stitch.
• The Olympus embroidery floss number follows each stitch; because Olympus floss is not widely available outside Japan, we have included the DMC floss number in parentheses.

Stitch Lesson 1

Tips for Beautifully Finished Contours

For some designs, it is important to achieve clean and crisp borders on specific areas, such as the bustier of the dress below. Take each stitch carefully and precisely along the marked outline with the needle perpendicular to the fabric as you work.

Full-size lid top pattern for Jewelry Box (shown on p. 5). See p. 64 for remaining patterns.

*Use color 900 (DMC 310) floss for all stitches unless otherwise stated. Or instead of embroidery floss, consider using black rayon machine embroidery thread to add sheen.

2 mm faux pearl beads

String approximately 36 of the 2 mm faux pearl beads on two strands of similar-colored floss. Tie off; arrange on the fabric as shown and secure to the fabric with tiny stitches.

neckline:
outline stitch (2); two rows

shoulder:
outline stitch (1)

armholes:
outline stitch (2);
two rows

bustier: outline filling stitch (2);
use a large-eye needle
(see p. 61 for instructions)

outline stitch (1)

satin stitch (1);
S105 (DMC 5283)

outline stitch (1)

satin stitch (1)

outline stitch (1);
S105 (DMC 5283)

lace: backstitch (2)
(see below for instructions).
Make the stitches a little uneven to give the impression of texture.

Stitch Lesson 2

How to Create the Lace for the Skirt

While appearing to be difficult, creating the effect of lace is quite simple if you follow these tips. Begin by dividing the skirt into five sections (A to E); delineate the folds using the outline stitch as shown. Draw squiggly lines vertically within each skirt section and backstitch them. Using these as a guide, begin to fill in around the squiggles close together, sometimes overlapping lines, but staying within each section of the skirt.

Jewelry box

shown on page **5**

Materials needed

Linen (lid top, bottom exterior, box band exterior, lid band exterior), 100 x 20 cm [40" x 8"]
Striped lining (lid lining, box band interior), 70 x 15 cm [28" x 6"]
Velvet (box bottom interior), 25 x 20 cm [10" x 8"]
Batting, 40 x 15 cm [16" x 6"]
Cardboard
  (2 mm thick), 40 x 15 cm [16" x 6"];
  (1 mm thick), 55 x 30 cm [22" x 12"];
  (0.5 mm thick), 55 x 5 cm [22" x 2"]
Gummed paper tape (the glue on the back is activated with water), 2.5 cm [1"] x length necessary for application
White craft glue
Embroidery (lid); see p. 44

1. Cutting cardboard pieces:

• The embroidery motifs and lid top pattern are on p. 44. Remaining full-size patterns (lid lining, box bottom, box bottom interior, and box bottom exterior) are on p. 64.
• Cut one of each piece.
• Using the measurements shown below, draw lines on the cardboard and cut out box band pieces.

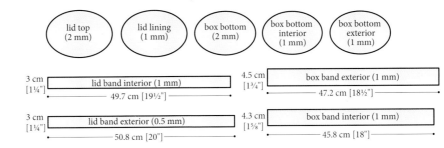

lid top (2 mm)
lid lining (1 mm)
box bottom (2 mm)
box bottom interior (1 mm)
box bottom exterior (1 mm)

3 cm [1¼"] — lid band interior (1 mm) — 49.7 cm [19½"]
4.5 cm [1¾"] — box band exterior (1 mm) — 47.2 cm [18½"]

3 cm [1¼"] — lid band exterior (0.5 mm) — 50.8 cm [20"]
4.3 cm [1⅝"] — box band interior (1 mm) — 45.8 cm [18"]

2. Cutting fabric pieces:

• Add seam allowances as shown to the lid top, lid lining, box bottom exterior, and box bottom interior patterns and cut out.
• Cut one of each fabric piece; cut two batting pieces.
• Using the measurements shown below, draw lines on the fabric and cut out the box band pieces.

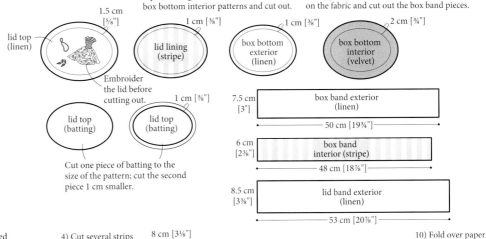

1.5 cm [⅝"]
lid top (linen)
Embroider the lid before cutting out.

1 cm [⅜"]
lid lining (stripe)

1 cm [⅜"]
box bottom exterior (linen)

2 cm [¾"]
box bottom interior (velvet)

1 cm [⅜"]
lid top (batting)
lid top (batting)
Cut one piece of batting to the size of the pattern; cut the second piece 1 cm smaller.

7.5 cm [3"] — box band exterior (linen) — 50 cm [19¾"]
6 cm [2⅜"] — box band interior (stripe) — 48 cm [18⅞"]
8.5 cm [3⅜"] — lid band exterior (linen) — 53 cm [20⅞"]

3. Assembling the box:

1) Apply glue on the thick part of the cardboard and match the edges flush against each other.

Glue

2) Affix gummed paper tape to where the edges meet.

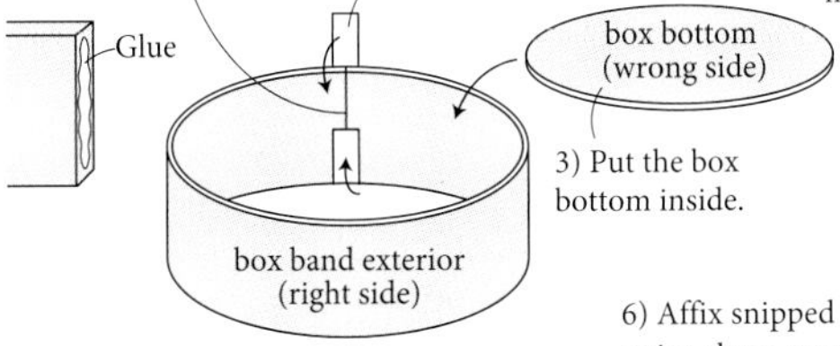

3) Put the box bottom inside.

box bottom (wrong side)

box band exterior (right side)

4) Cut several strips of gummed paper tape and make alternating snips into the edges.

8 cm [3⅛"]
1.5 cm [⅝"]

5) Apply glue where pieces meet.

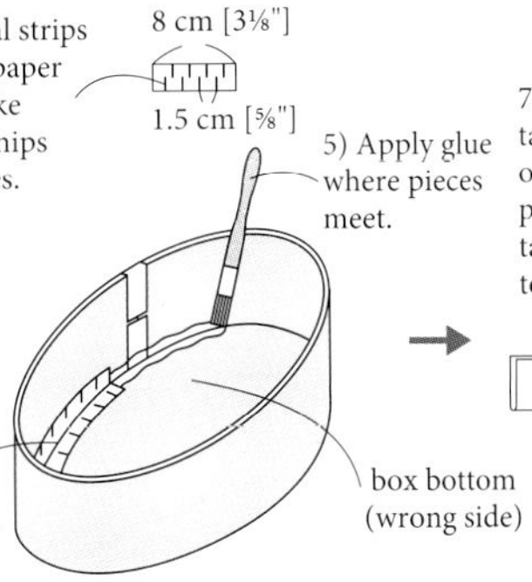

6) Affix snipped paper tape strips along curves to firmly secure pieces together.

box bottom (wrong side)

7) Cut a strip of paper tape to the length of the outer circumference plus 1 cm [⅝"]. Fold the tape in half lengthwise to make a crease.

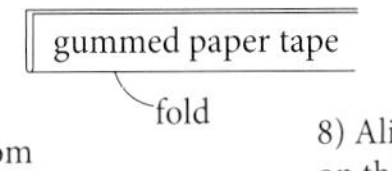

gummed paper tape
fold

8) Align the crease on the paper tape with the rim and secure the tape around the rim.

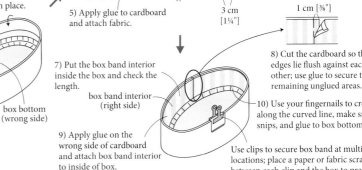

10) Fold over paper tape and press in place.

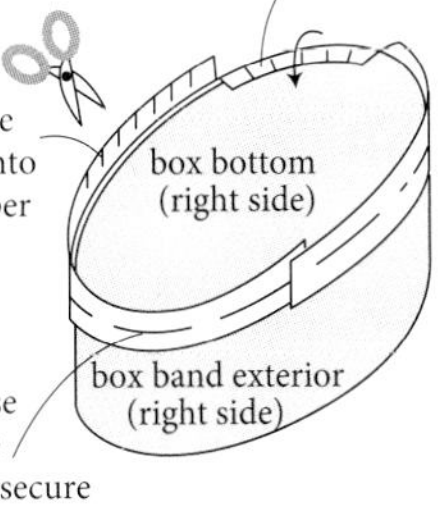

9) Make snips into the paper tape.

box bottom (right side)

box band exterior (right side)

4. Gluing the box band exterior and interior to the box:

1) Apply glue on the box band exterior and attach the box band exterior fabric to the box band exterior.

2) Make snips to within 0.3 cm [⅛"] from the edge.

3) Apply glue along the rim of the box bottom, fold over the fabric, and finger-press in place.

1.5 cm [⅝"]
0.3 cm [⅛"]

box bottom (right side)

box band exterior (right side)

Overlap edges by 1 cm [⅜"].
Fold under by 1 cm [⅜"].

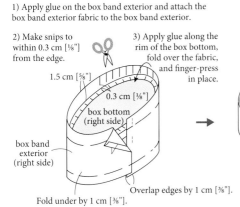

4) Apply glue along the inner rim of the box, fold over the fabric, and press in place.

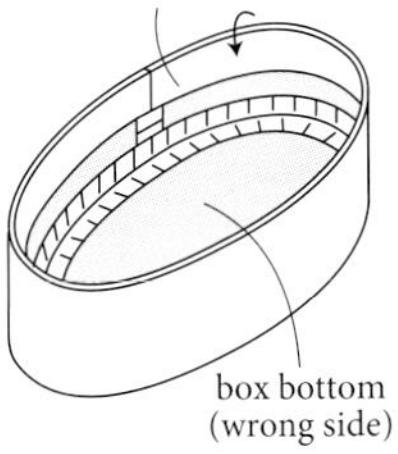

box bottom (wrong side)

6) Apply glue along seam allowances on two sides and fold over cardboard.

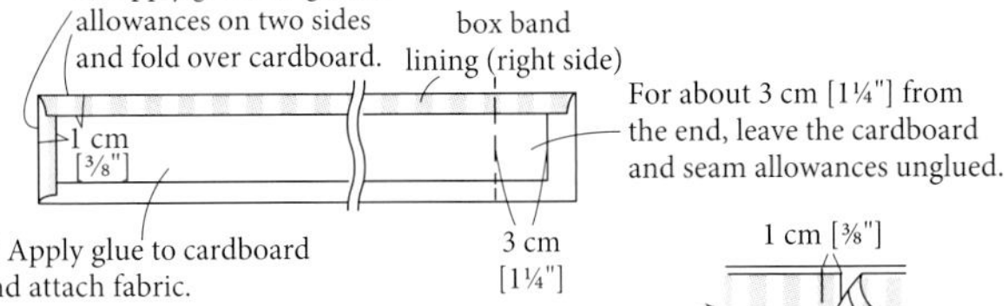

box band lining (right side)

1 cm [⅜"]
3 cm [1¼"]

5) Apply glue to cardboard and attach fabric.

For about 3 cm [1¼"] from the end, leave the cardboard and seam allowances unglued.

1 cm [⅜"]

7) Put the box band interior inside the box and check the length.

box band interior (right side)

8) Cut the cardboard so the edges lie flush against each other; use glue to secure the remaining unglued areas.

9) Apply glue on the wrong side of cardboard and attach box band interior to inside of box.

10) Use your fingernails to crease along the curved line, make small snips, and glue to box bottom interior.

Use clips to secure box band at multiple locations; place a paper or fabric scrap between each clip and the box to prevent the clip from making a mark.

5. Making and attaching the bottom interior and exterior:

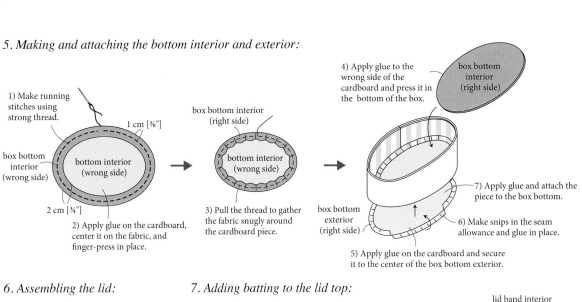

1) Make running stitches using strong thread.

1 cm [⅜"]

box bottom interior (right side)

box bottom interior (wrong side)

bottom interior (wrong side)

2 cm [¾"]

2) Apply glue on the cardboard, center it on the fabric, and finger-press in place.

3) Pull the thread to gather the fabric snugly around the cardboard piece.

bottom interior (wrong side)

4) Apply glue to the wrong side of the cardboard and press it in the bottom of the box.

box bottom interior (right side)

7) Apply glue and attach the piece to the box bottom.

box bottom exterior (right side)

6) Make snips in the seam allowance and glue in place.

5) Apply glue on the cardboard and secure it to the center of the box bottom exterior.

6. Assembling the lid:

Refer to instructions for assembling the box on p. 45 and assemble in the same manner.

lid top (right side)

gummed paper tape

lid band interior (right side)

7. Adding batting to the lid top:

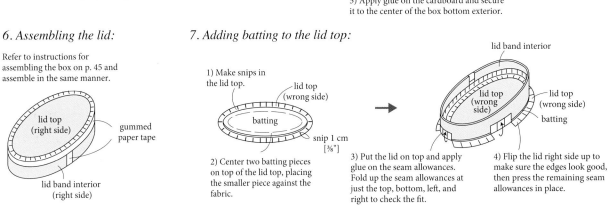

1) Make snips in the lid top.

lid top (wrong side)

batting

snip 1 cm [⅜"]

2) Center two batting pieces on top of the lid top, placing the smaller piece against the fabric.

lid band interior

lid top (wrong side)

lid top (wrong side)

batting

3) Put the lid on top and apply glue on the seam allowances. Fold up the seam allowances at just the top, bottom, left, and right to check the fit.

4) Flip the lid right side up to make sure the edges look good, then press the remaining seam allowances in place.

8. Attaching box band to the lid:

1) Fold down 3 cm [1¼"] (same as the width of the lid band exterior).

lid band exterior (wrong side)

2) Apply glue on the cardboard, fold over the fabric, and press in place.

lid band exterior (wrong side)

0.5 cm [¼"]

(right side)

3) Fold under and glue one end.

lid band exterior (wrong side)

3 cm [1¼"]

Do not apply glue here.

4) Wrap the box band around the lid to check the length.

lid top (right side)

5) Without cutting the fabric, cut the cardboard in the box band so the ends lie flush against each other, and use glue to secure the remaining unglued areas.

lid band exterior (right side)

overlap by 1 cm [⅜"]

6) Apply glue on the wrong side and wrap around the lid.

9. Attaching lid lining to the lid:

1) Apply glue on the right side of the cardboard and glue the lid lining in place.

lid lining (wrong side)

lid lining (wrong side)

1.5 cm [⅝"]

2) Make snips in the seam allowance.

3) Apply glue on the seam allowance, fold over, and press in place.

(4) Apply glue on the wrong side of the cardboard, put it in the bottom of the lid, and press in place.

lid lining (right side)

7) Apply glue to inside of the lid and tuck down the fabric.

8) Use your nails to trace the corners, follow the curved line, and shape the lid.

9) Make snips in the seam allowance and glue in place.

lid top (wrong side)

lid band exterior (right side)

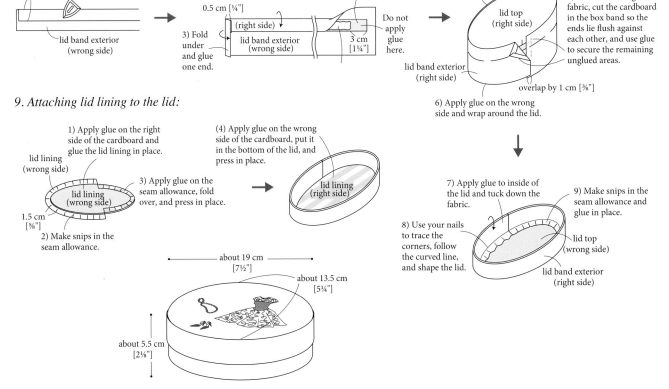

about 19 cm [7½"]

about 13.5 cm [5¼"]

about 5.5 cm [2⅛"]

Favorite things

shown on pages 6, 7

• The full-size Favorite Things embroidery patterns are below.
• The number in the parentheses stands for the number of strands used for the specific stitch.
• The Olympus embroidery floss number follows each stitch; because Olympus floss is not widely available outside Japan, we have included the DMC floss number in parentheses.

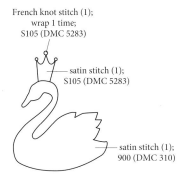

French knot stitch (1); wrap 1 time; S105 (DMC 5283)

satin stitch (1); S105 (DMC 5283)

satin stitch (1); 900 (DMC 310)

Black Swan

satin stitch (1); 486 (DMC 414)

satin stitch (1); 731 (DMC 712)

shoes, ribbon: satin stitch (1); 900 (DMC 310)

toe area: double satin stitch (2); 900 (DMC 310) (see p. 58 for instructions)

Ballet Shoes

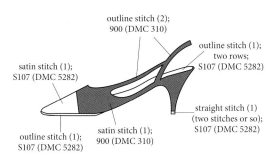

outline stitch (2); 900 (DMC 310)

outline stitch (1); two rows; S107 (DMC 5282)

satin stitch (1); S107 (DMC 5282)

straight stitch (1) (two stitches or so); S107 (DMC 5282)

outline stitch (1); S107 (DMC 5282)

satin stitch (1); 900 (DMC 310)

Strappy Heels

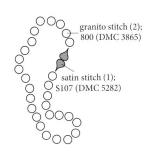

granito stitch (2); 800 (DMC 3865)

satin stitch (1); S107 (DMC 5282)

Pearl Necklace

Stitch Lesson 3

Embroidering the Granito Stitch, also called the Dot Stitch

1. The needle comes out from the back at (1), goes down into the fabric at (2); back out of the fabric at (3), which is the same location as (1).

2. The needle goes down into the fabric at (4), which is the same location as (2), and back out of the fabric at (5), which is the same location as (1).

3. Continue stitching in and out of the same holes to make a dot. Follow the contour of the motif, working outer stitches loosely.

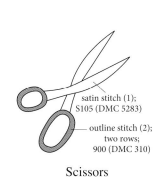

satin stitch (1); S105 (DMC 5283)

outline stitch (2); two rows; 900 (DMC 310)

Scissors

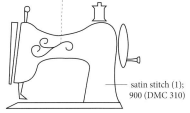

To prepare a couching thread, unravel one strand of embroidery floss to make a fine thread.

Switch to just one strand for the remainder; S107 (DMC 5282)

Use two strands for the first area; S107 (DMC 5282)

couching stitch

Start here.

satin stitch (1); 900 (DMC 310)

Sewing Machine

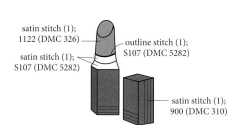

satin stitch (1); 1122 (DMC 326)

satin stitch (1); S107 (DMC 5282)

outline stitch (1); S107 (DMC 5282)

satin stitch (1); 900 (DMC 310)

Lipstick

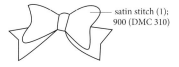

satin stitch (1); 900 (DMC 310)

Ribbon & Bow

Lace lingerie

shown on page 10

- The full-size Lace Lingerie embroidery patterns are below.
- The number in the parentheses stands for the number of strands used for the specific stitch.
- The Olympus embroidery floss number follows each stitch; because Olympus floss is not widely available outside Japan, we have included the DMC floss number in parentheses.

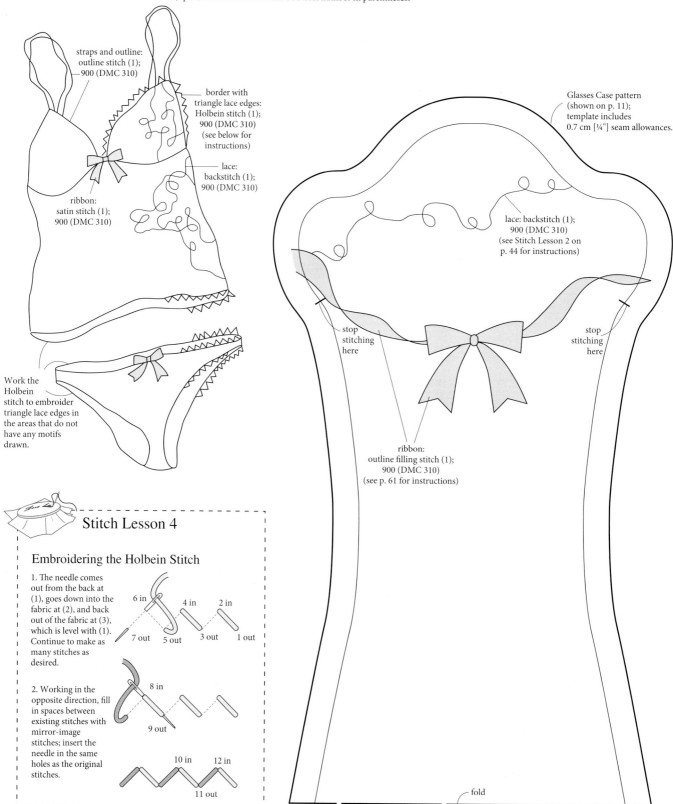

straps and outline:
outline stitch (1);
900 (DMC 310)

border with
triangle lace edges:
Holbein stitch (1);
900 (DMC 310)
(see below for
instructions)

lace:
backstitch (1);
900 (DMC 310)

ribbon:
satin stitch (1);
900 (DMC 310)

Work the
Holbein
stitch to embroider
triangle lace edges
in the areas that do not
have any motifs
drawn.

Glasses Case pattern
(shown on p. 11);
template includes
0.7 cm [¼"] seam allowances.

lace: backstitch (1);
900 (DMC 310)
(see Stitch Lesson 2 on
p. 44 for instructions)

stop
stitching
here

stop
stitching
here

ribbon:
outline filling stitch (1);
900 (DMC 310)
(see p. 61 for instructions)

fold

Stitch Lesson 4

Embroidering the Holbein Stitch

1. The needle comes out from the back at (1), goes down into the fabric at (2), and back out of the fabric at (3), which is level with (1). Continue to make as many stitches as desired.

6 in   4 in   2 in
7 out   5 out   3 out   1 out

2. Working in the opposite direction, fill in spaces between existing stitches with mirror-image stitches; insert the needle in the same holes as the original stitches.

8 in
9 out

10 in   12 in
11 out

Glasses case

shown on page **11**

Materials needed

Linen (case exterior), 15 x 40 cm [5¾" x 15¾"]
Striped fabric (case lining), 15 x 40 cm [5¾" x 15¾"]
Interfacing, 30 x 40 cm [11¾" x 15¾"]
Batting, 15 x 40 cm [5¾" x 15¾"]
Embroidery floss: black

1. Embroidering the case and cutting fabric pieces:

- The embroidery motif and full-size pattern are on p. 48.
- Cut interfacing into two 15 x 40 cm [5¾" x 15¾"] pieces.
- Cut one pattern from from batting.

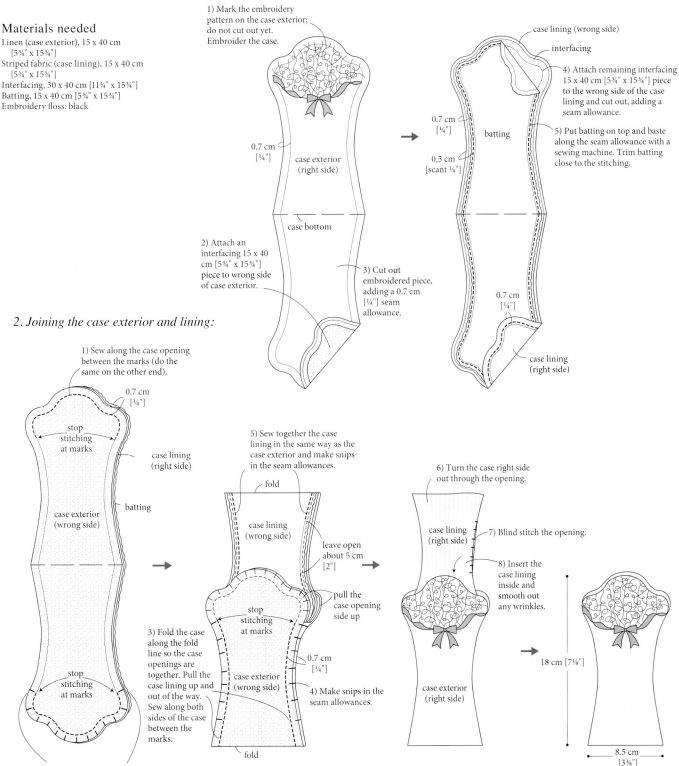

1) Mark the embroidery pattern on the case exterior; do not cut out yet. Embroider the case.

2) Attach an interfacing 15 x 40 cm [5¾" x 15¾"] piece to wrong side of case exterior.

3) Cut out embroidered piece, adding a 0.7 cm [¼"] seam allowance.

0.7 cm [¼"]

case exterior (right side)

case bottom

case lining (wrong side)

interfacing

4) Attach remaining interfacing 15 x 40 cm [5¾" x 15¾"] piece to the wrong side of the case lining and cut out, adding a seam allowance.

5) Put batting on top and baste along the seam allowance with a sewing machine. Trim batting close to the stitching.

0.7 cm [¼"]

0.5 cm [scant ¼"]

batting

0.7 cm [¼"]

case lining (right side)

2. Joining the case exterior and lining:

1) Sew along the case opening between the marks (do the same on the other end).

0.7 cm [¼"]

stop stitching at marks

case lining (right side)

case exterior (wrong side)

batting

stop stitching at marks

2) Trim the seam allowances along the case opening to 0.5 cm [a scant ¼"] and make snips (do the same on the other end).

3) Fold the case along the fold line so the case openings are together. Pull the case lining up and out of the way. Sew along both sides of the case between the marks.

5) Sew together the case lining in the same way as the case exterior and make snips in the seam allowances.

fold

case lining (wrong side)

leave open about 5 cm [2"]

pull the case opening side up

stop stitching at marks

0.7 cm [¼"]

case exterior (wrong side)

4) Make snips in the seam allowances.

fold

6) Turn the case right side out through the opening.

case lining (right side)

7) Blind stitch the opening.

8) Insert the case lining inside and smooth out any wrinkles.

case exterior (right side)

18 cm [7⅛"]

8.5 cm [3⅜"]

Violets

shown on page **12**

- The full-size Violets embroidery patterns are below.
- The number in the parentheses stands for the number of strands used for the specific stitch.
- The Olympus embroidery floss number follows each stitch; because Olympus floss is not widely available outside Japan, we have included the DMC floss number in parentheses.

flower petals: satin stitch (2).
Choose four different tones of a color for each of the flower petals A, B, C, and D:
A = 605 (DMC 550)
B = 603 (DMC 552)
C = 674 (DMC 553)
D = 673 (DMC 554)

flower centers:
French knot stitch (2);
wrap one time;
134 (DMC 718)

leaves, calyx:
satin stitch (2)

stems:
backstitch (2)

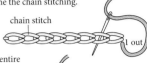

Stitch Lesson 5

Embroidering the Wrapped Chain Stitch

1. Make a chain stitch the desired length. Thread the needle with a contrasting color of floss and bring it out at (1). Insert the floss behind the next loop of the the chain stitching.

chain stitch

1 out

2. Repeat the entire length of the chain stitching. Bring the thread to the back and secure.

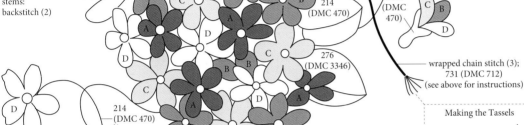

all remaining stems 214 (DMC 470)

218 (DMC 469)

276 (DMC 3346)

218 (DMC 469)

218 (DMC 469)

214 (DMC 470)

214 (DMC 470)

214 (DMC 470)

276 (DMC 3346)

wrapped chain stitch (3);
731 (DMC 712)
(see above for instructions)

218 (DMC 469)

Making the Tassels

wrapped chain stitch

Cut a 4 cm [1½"] length of six strands of 731 (DMC 712) floss; fold in half; secure with a couple stitches.

Use three strands of 731 (DMC 712) floss; wrap and stitch around the folded center several times; secure.

Round petit box

shown on page **9**

Materials needed

See individual embroidery motifs on p. 47 for information on embroidery threads.
Linen (lid top, lid band, box band exterior, box bottom interior), 20 x 15 cm [8" x 6"]
Printed fabric (lid lining, box band interior, box bottom interior), 15 x 10 cm [6" x 4"]
Cardboard
 (1 mm thick), 15 x 10 cm [6" x 4"];
 (0.5 mm thick), 15 x 10 cm [6" x 4"]
White craft glue

3. Finishing the box:

Refer to steps 3 through 6 of the instructions for the Oval Petit Box on p. 70 to finish the box.

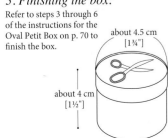

about 4.5 cm [1¾"]

about 4 cm [1½"]

1. Cutting cardboard pieces:

- The full-size patterns are on p. 64.
- Cut one of each piece.
- Using the measurements shown below, draw lines on the cardboard and cut out box band pieces.

lid top (1 mm)

lid lining (0.5 mm)

box bottom (1 mm)

box bottom interior (0.5 mm)

box bottom exterior (0.5 mm)

3.5 cm [1⅜"]

box band exterior (1 mm)

— 12 cm [4¾"] —

3 cm [1¼"]

box band interior (0.5 mm)

— 11 cm [4⅜"] —

1 cm [⅜"]

lid band (1 mm)

— 12.8 cm [5"] —

2. Cutting fabric pieces:

- Add seam allowances as shown to the lid and box bottom patterns and cut out.
- Cut one of each fabric piece.
- Using the measurements shown below, draw lines on the fabric and cut out box band pieces.

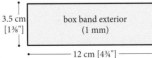

Lid top (linen)

0.5 cm [¼"]

0.5 cm [¼"]

lid lining (printed fabric)

0.5 cm [¼"]

box bottom exterior (linen)

0.5 cm [¼"]

box bottom interior (printed fabric)

Embroider the lid before cutting out.

5.5 cm [2⅛"]

box band exterior (linen)

— 14.5 cm [5⅝"] —

5 cm [2"]

lid band exterior (linen)

— 15.5 cm [6⅛"] —

5 cm [2"]

box band interior (patterned fabric)

— 13 cm [5⅛"] —

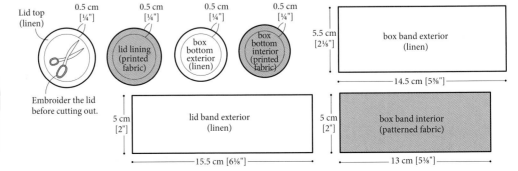

Chamomile

shown on page 14

- The full-size Chamomile embroidery patterns are below.
- The number in the parentheses stands for the number of strands used for the specific stitch.
- The Olympus embroidery floss number follows each stitch; because Olympus floss is not widely available outside Japan, we have included the DMC floss number in parentheses.

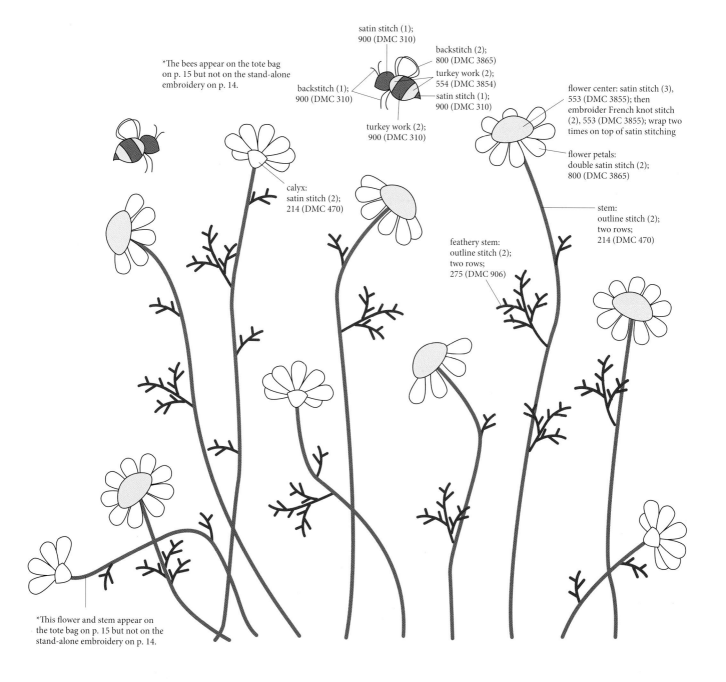

satin stitch (1); 900 (DMC 310)

backstitch (2); 800 (DMC 3865)

turkey work (2); 554 (DMC 3854)

satin stitch (1); 900 (DMC 310)

*The bees appear on the tote bag on p. 15 but not on the stand-alone embroidery on p. 14.

backstitch (1); 900 (DMC 310)

turkey work (2); 900 (DMC 310)

flower center: satin stitch (3), 553 (DMC 3855); then embroider French knot stitch (2), 553 (DMC 3855); wrap two times on top of satin stitching

flower petals: double satin stitch (2); 800 (DMC 3865)

calyx: satin stitch (2); 214 (DMC 470)

stem: outline stitch (2); two rows; 214 (DMC 470)

feathery stem: outline stitch (2); two rows; 275 (DMC 906)

*This flower and stem appear on the tote bag on p. 15 but not on the stand-alone embroidery on p. 14.

Hollyhocks

- The full-size Hollyhocks embroidery patterns are below.
- The number in the parentheses stands for the number of strands used for the specific stitch.
- The Olympus embroidery floss number follows each stitch; because Olympus floss is not widely available outside Japan, we have included the DMC floss number in parentheses.

flowers: buttonhole stitch

flower buds: French knot stitch (wrap one to two times)

leaves: after stitching the leaves, backstitch the outlines

stems: outline stitch (2) for all areas

* Use two strands for all areas unless otherwise stated by another number in parentheses.

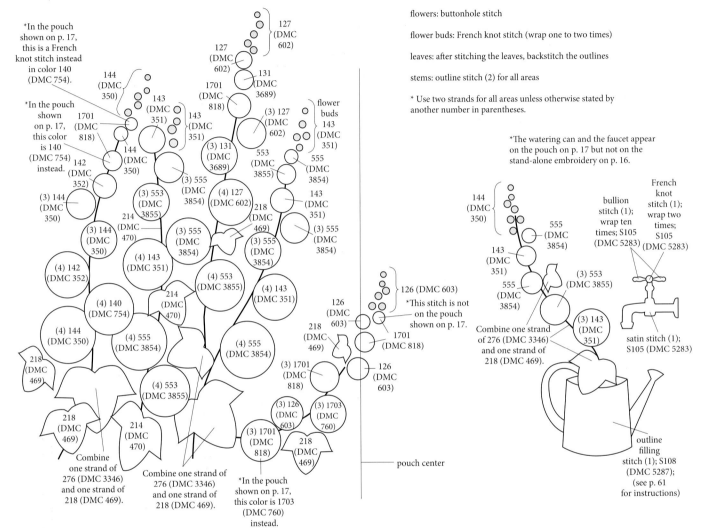

*The watering can and the faucet appear on the pouch on p. 17 but not on the stand-alone embroidery on p. 16.

Stitch Lesson 6

Embroidering the Leaf Stitch

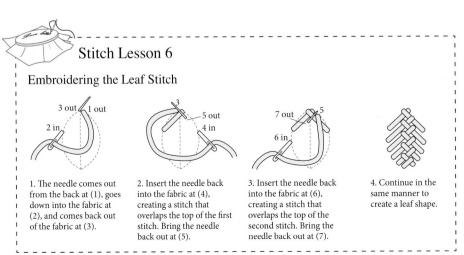

1. The needle comes out from the back at (1), goes down into the fabric at (2), and comes back out of the fabric at (3).

2. Insert the needle back into the fabric at (4), creating a stitch that overlaps the top of the first stitch. Bring the needle back out at (5).

3. Insert the needle back into the fabric at (6), creating a stitch that overlaps the top of the second stitch. Bring the needle back out at (7).

4. Continue in the same manner to create a leaf shape.

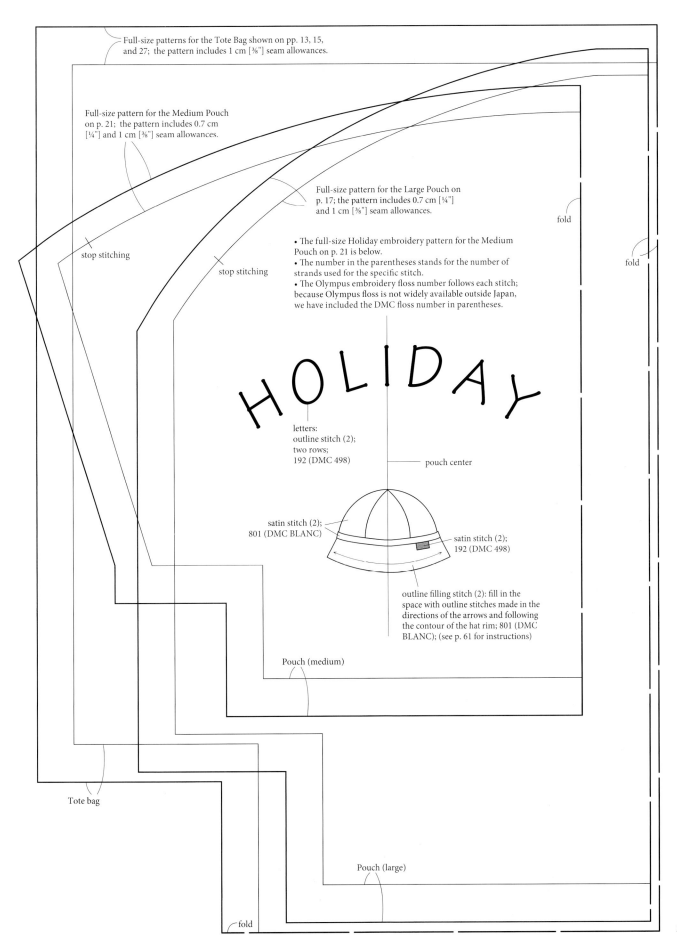

Full-size patterns for the Tote Bag shown on pp. 13, 15, and 27; the pattern includes 1 cm [⅜"] seam allowances.

Full-size pattern for the Medium Pouch on p. 21; the pattern includes 0.7 cm [¼"] and 1 cm [⅜"] seam allowances.

Full-size pattern for the Large Pouch on p. 17; the pattern includes 0.7 cm [¼"] and 1 cm [⅜"] seam allowances.

fold

fold

• The full-size Holiday embroidery pattern for the Medium Pouch on p. 21 is below.
• The number in the parentheses stands for the number of strands used for the specific stitch.
• The Olympus embroidery floss number follows each stitch; because Olympus floss is not widely available outside Japan, we have included the DMC floss number in parentheses.

stop stitching

stop stitching

HOLIDAY

letters:
outline stitch (2);
two rows;
192 (DMC 498)

pouch center

satin stitch (2);
801 (DMC BLANC)

satin stitch (2);
192 (DMC 498)

outline filling stitch (2): fill in the space with outline stitches made in the directions of the arrows and following the contour of the hat rim; 801 (DMC BLANC); (see p. 61 for instructions)

Pouch (medium)

Tote bag

Pouch (large)

fold

Climbing Roses

shown on page **18**

- The full-size Climbing Roses embroidery patterns are below.
- To embroider the project on p. 18, trace the pattern as is onto a single piece of fabric.
- To embroider the pocket board on p. 19, divide and trace the pattern according to the specified locations (see instructions).
- The number in the parentheses stands for the number of strands used for the specific stitch.
- The Olympus embroidery floss number follows each stitch; because Olympus floss is not widely available outside Japan, we have included the DMC floss number in parentheses.

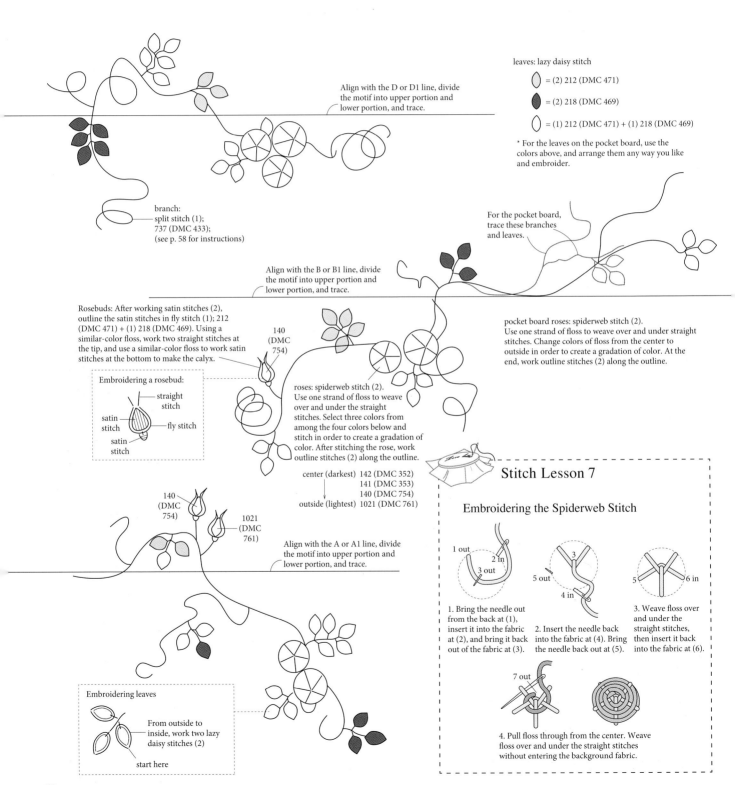

Align with the D or D1 line, divide the motif into upper portion and lower portion, and trace.

leaves: lazy daisy stitch

= (2) 212 (DMC 471)

= (2) 218 (DMC 469)

= (1) 212 (DMC 471) + (1) 218 (DMC 469)

* For the leaves on the pocket board, use the colors above, and arrange them any way you like and embroider.

branch:
split stitch (1);
737 (DMC 433);
(see p. 58 for instructions)

For the pocket board, trace these branches and leaves.

Align with the B or B1 line, divide the motif into upper portion and lower portion, and trace.

Rosebuds: After working satin stitches (2), outline the satin stitches in fly stitch (1); 212 (DMC 471) + (1) 218 (DMC 469). Using a similar-color floss, work two straight stitches at the tip, and use a similar-color floss to work satin stitches at the bottom to make the calyx.

140 (DMC 754)

roses: spiderweb stitch (2).
Use one strand of floss to weave over and under the straight stitches. Select three colors from among the four colors below and stitch in order to create a gradation of color. After stitching the rose, work outline stitches (2) along the outline.

pocket board roses: spiderweb stitch (2).
Use one strand of floss to weave over and under straight stitches. Change colors of floss from the center to outside in order to create a gradation of color. At the end, work outline stitches (2) along the outline.

center (darkest) 142 (DMC 352)
141 (DMC 353)
140 (DMC 754)
outside (lightest) 1021 (DMC 761)

Embroidering a rosebud:

straight stitch
satin stitch
fly stitch
satin stitch

140 (DMC 754)

1021 (DMC 761)

Align with the A or A1 line, divide the motif into upper portion and lower portion, and trace.

Stitch Lesson 7

Embroidering the Spiderweb Stitch

1 out
2 in
3 out

1. Bring the needle out from the back at (1), insert it into the fabric at (2), and bring it back out of the fabric at (3).

3
5 out
4 in

2. Insert the needle back into the fabric at (4). Bring the needle back out at (5).

5
6 in

3. Weave floss over and under the straight stitches, then insert it back into the fabric at (6).

7 out

4. Pull floss through from the center. Weave floss over and under the straight stitches without entering the background fabric.

Embroidering leaves

From outside to inside, work two lazy daisy stitches (2)

start here

Pocket board

shown on page **19**

Materials needed

See individual embroidery motifs on p. 54 for information on embroidery threads.

Linen (pocket fabric, backing), 70 cm x 1 m [27½" x 39"]

Plywood panel (1.2 cm [½"] thick), 25 x 32 cm [9¾" x 12⅝"]

Grosgrain ribbon (1.5 cm [⅝"] wide), 120 cm [47"]

White craft glue

1. Cutting and marking fabric pieces:

- The embroidery motifs are on p. 54.
- Cut one of each fabric piece.
- Using the measurements shown below, draw lines on the fabric and cut out pieces.

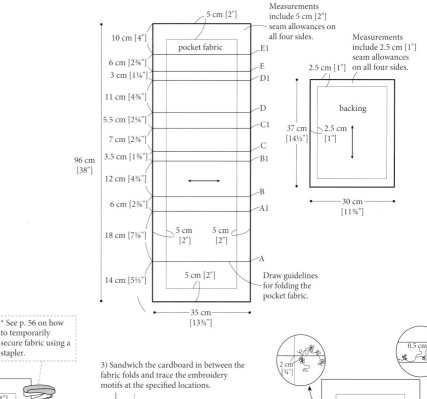

Measurements include 5 cm [2"] seam allowances on all four sides.

5 cm [2"]

10 cm [4"]

pocket fabric — E1

6 cm [2⅜"] — E

3 cm [1¼"] — D1

11 cm [4⅜"] — D

5.5 cm [2⅛"] — C1

7 cm [2¾"] — C

3.5 cm [1⅜"] — B1

12 cm [4¾"] — B

6 cm [2⅜"] — A1

18 cm [7⅛"]

5 cm [2"]   5 cm [2"]

— A

14 cm [5½"]   5 cm [2"]   Draw guidelines for folding the pocket fabric.

96 cm [38"]

35 cm [13¾"]

Measurements include 2.5 cm [1"] seam allowances on all four sides.

2.5 cm [1"]

backing

37 cm [14½"]   2.5 cm [1"]

30 cm [11¾"]

2. Folding and embroidering pockets:

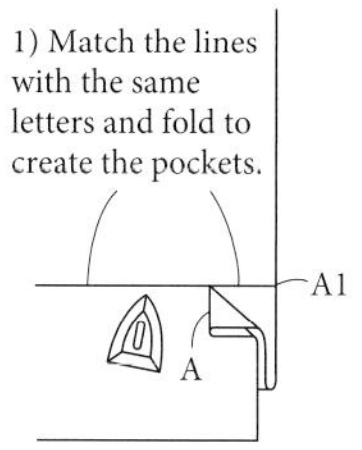

* See p. 56 on how to temporarily secure fabric using a stapler.

1) Match the lines with the same letters and fold to create the pockets.

A1

A

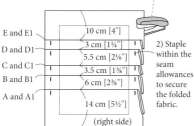

E and E1   10 cm [4"]
D and D1   3 cm [1¼"]
           5.5 cm [2⅛"]
C and C1   3.5 cm [1⅜"]
B and B1   6 cm [2⅜"]
A and A1   14 cm [5½"]

2) Staple within the seam allowances to secure the folded fabric.

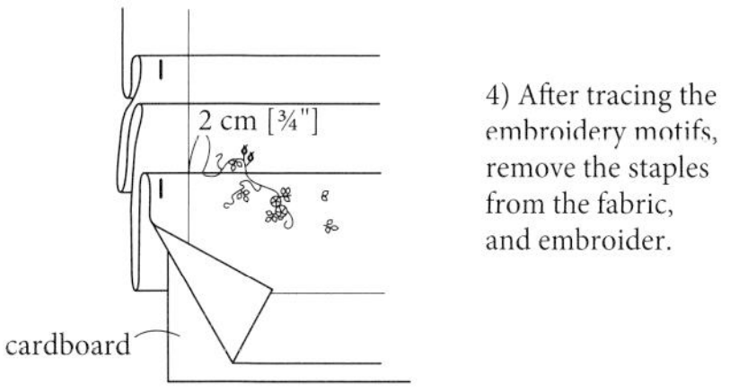

(right side)

3) Sandwich the cardboard in between the fabric folds and trace the embroidery motifs at the specified locations.

2 cm [¾"]

cardboard

4) After tracing the embroidery motifs, remove the staples from the fabric, and embroider.

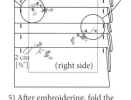

0.5 cm [¼"]

2 cm [¾"]

2 cm [¾"]   (right side)

5) After embroidering, fold the fabric, and use a stapler to secure the fabric as done in step 2.

3. Wrapping plywood with pocket fabric:

1) Place the plywood panel on top of the pocket fabric.

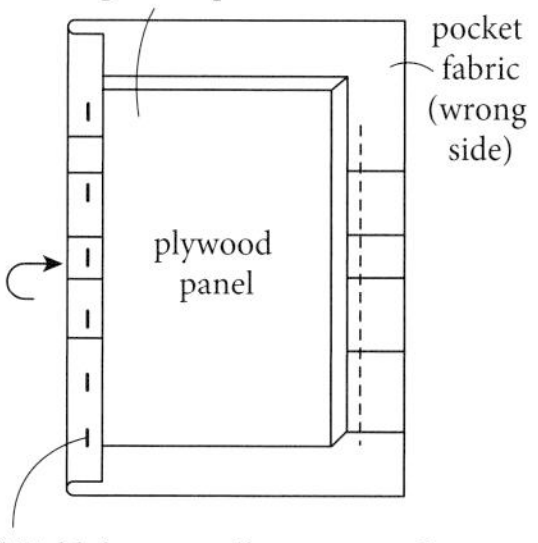

plywood panel

pocket fabric (wrong side)

2) Fold the seam allowances to the back on right and left sides and secure them with a staple gun.

3) Fold the seam allowances to the back at the top and bottom.

plywood panel

* When folding the top and bottom sides to the back, be careful with the tension of the fabric so the pockets are not pulled open.

To secure fabric to a wooden board, use a staple gun. Similar to staplers, staple guns are used to drive heavy metal staples into wood, etc., to secure fabric or paper. Staple guns are useful in many DIY situations so it is convenient to have one in your craft room.

4. Attaching backing fabric:

1) Fold under and press the seam allowances on the backing piece.

2.5 cm [1"]

2.5 cm [1"]   backing (wrong side)   2.5 cm [1"]

2.5 cm [1"]

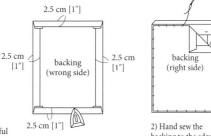

backing (right side)

2) Hand sew the backing to the edges of the pocket-covered plywood panel.

5. Attaching ribbons:

1) Apply glue to the panel edges and attach the grosgrain ribbon to cover the edges.

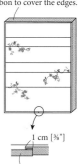

1 cm [⅜"]

2) Fold under one ribbon end. Lap the folded end over the unfinished ribbon end.

Medium pouch

shown on page **21**

Materials needed

See individual embroidery motifs on pp. 53 and 59 for information on embroidery threads.

Linen (pouch exterior), 65 x 20 cm [26" x 8"]
Printed fabric (pouch lining), 65 x 20 cm [26" x 8"]
Interfacing, 90 x 40 cm [36" x 16"]
Zipper, 28 cm long [11" long]
Board for the bottom (thin cardboard or plastic), 17.5 x 6 cm [6⅞" x 2⅜"]
Faux leather (tassel), 8 x 3 cm [3⅛" x 1¼"]
Heavy-duty double-sided tape
White craft glue
Embroidery floss to match the faux leather

1. Embroidering and cutting fabric pieces:

- The full-size pattern is on p. 53.
- Embroidery patterns are on pp. 53 and 59.

1) Embroider the pouch exterior using the desired motif.

pouch exterior (right side)

HOLIDAY see p. 53

6.5 cm [2⅝"]

pouch exterior (wrong side)

VACATION see p. 59

6.5 cm [2⅝"]

2) Attach interfacing on the wrong side and cut out two pouch exterior pieces.

3) Attach interfacing on the wrong side and cut out two pouch lining pieces.

pouch lining (right side)

pouch lining (wrong side)   interfacing

2. Inserting the zipper:

1) Baste the zipper in place.

zipper (wrong side)

HOLIDAY

pouch exterior (right side)

2) Put the pouch lining on top, sandwiching the zipper. Sew through all layers.

0.7 cm [¼"]

stop stitching   stop stitching

pouch lining (wrong side)

pouch exterior (right side)

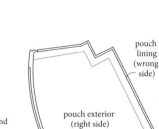

pouch lining (wrong side)

pouch exterior (right side)

3) Turn right side out and smooth out any wrinkles.

4) In the same manner, sew together the pouch exterior and lining on the other side of the zipper.

pouch lining (wrong side)

HOLIDAY

pouch exterior (right side)

Sewing Lesson

seam line

Temporarily Securing Fabric

Pins or basting stitches are often used to temporarily secure a zipper or fabric pieces together. In this book, we recommend using a stapler. A household stapler capable of securing thick paper is used here. Staples firmly hold pieces together even along curved lines, where pinning is difficult. When using a stapler for this purpose, be sure not to put staples on the seam line so your sewing needle will not break. Always remember to remove the staples when you are finished sewing. Do not use staples on materials such as chiffon, organdy, or other thin fabric, because the staples can snag the woven threads.

3. Sewing pouch sides and bottom:

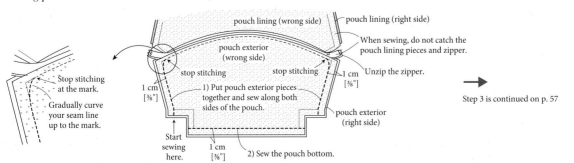

pouch lining (wrong side)   pouch lining (right side)

pouch exterior (wrong side)

When sewing, do not catch the pouch lining pieces and zipper.

stop stitching   stop stitching

Unzip the zipper.

1 cm [⅜"]

Stop stitching at the mark.

Gradually curve your seam line up to the mark.

1 cm [⅜"]

1) Put pouch exterior pieces together and sew along both sides of the pouch.

pouch exterior (right side)

Start sewing here.

1 cm [⅜"]

2) Sew the pouch bottom.

Step 3 is continued on p. 57

Large pouch

shown on page 17

Materials needed

See individual embroidery motifs on pp. 52, 53, and
    59 for information on embroidery threads.
Linen (pouch exterior), 60 x 25 cm [24" x 10"]
Printed fabric (pouch lining), 60 x 25 cm [24" x 10"]
Interfacing, 90 x 50 cm [36" x 20"]
Zipper, 26 cm long [10¼" long]
Board for the bottom (thin cardboard or plastic),
    18 x 8 cm [7¼" x 3⅛"]
Heavy-duty double sided tape
Embroidery floss: orange (tassel)

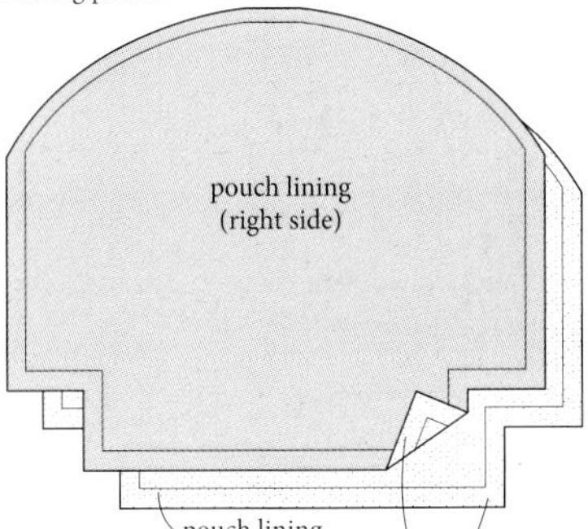

*2. Repeat steps 2 and 3 of instructions
for the Medium-Sized Pouch on p. 56.*

1. Embroidering and cutting fabric pieces:

- The full-size pattern is on p. 53.
- The embroidery pattern is on p. 52.

1) Embroider the pouch exterior.

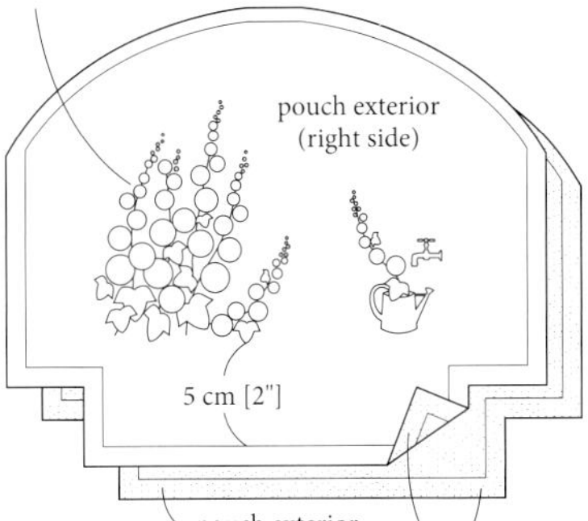

pouch exterior
(right side)

5 cm [2"]

pouch exterior
(wrong side)

2) Attach interfacing on the wrong side
and cut out two pouch exterior pieces.

3) Attach interfacing on the wrong side and cut out two
    pouch lining pieces.

pouch lining
(right side)

pouch lining
(wrong side)

interfacing

3. Finishing the pouch:

1) Attach heavy-duty
double-sided tape to the
board for the pouch bottom.

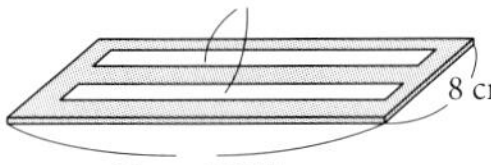

8 cm [3⅛"]
18 cm [7⅛"]

3) Blind stitch the opening.

pouch lining
(right side)

4) Put the
pouch lining
inside and
smooth out
any wrinkles.

pouch exterior
(right side)

16.5 cm
[6½"]

5) Make
and
attach a
tassel.

2) Turn the pouch right side
out. Insert the board into the
lining opening and adhere the
taped side of the board to the
bottom of the pouch exterior.

8 cm [3⅛"]
18 cm [7⅛"]

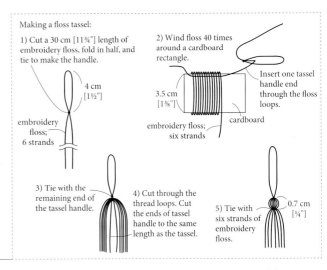

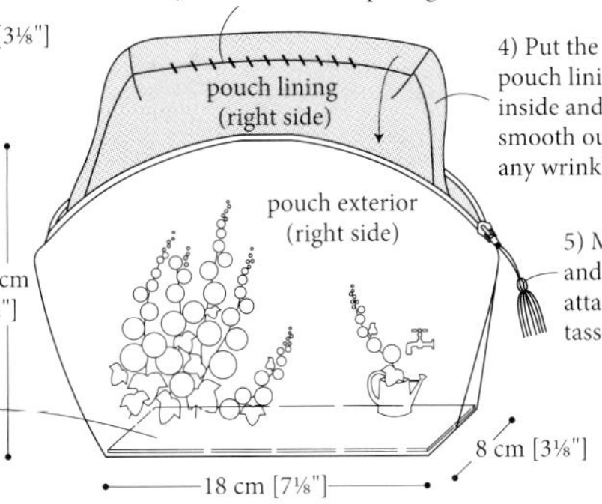

Making a floss tassel:

1) Cut a 30 cm [11¾"] length of
embroidery floss, fold in half, and
tie to make the handle.

4 cm
[1½"]

embroidery
floss;
6 strands

3) Tie with the
remaining end of
the tassel handle.

2) Wind floss 40 times
around a cardboard
rectangle.

Insert one tassel
handle end
through the floss
loops.

3.5 cm
[1⅜"]

embroidery floss;
six strands

cardboard

4) Cut through the
thread loops. Cut
the ends of tassel
handle to the same
length as the tassel.

5) Tie with
six strands of
embroidery
floss.

0.7 cm
[¼"]

Step 3 continued from p. 56

pouch exterior (wrong side)

3) Put pouch lining pieces
together and sew along
both sides of the pouch.

1 cm
[⅜"]

pouch lining (wrong side)

pouch lining
(right side)

4) Sew the pouch bottom

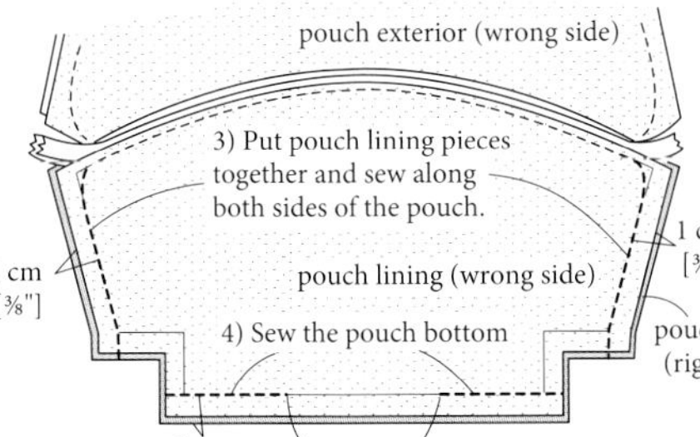

1 cm
[⅜"]

1 cm
[⅜"]

leave open 10 to 12 cm [4" to 4¾"]

4. Sewing the gussets:

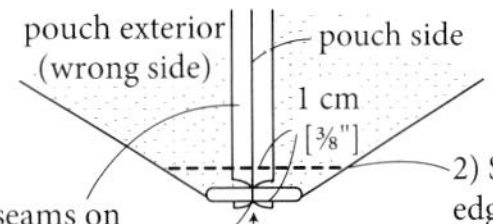

pouch exterior
(wrong side)

pouch side

1 cm
[⅜"]

1) Open the seams on
the side and pouch
bottom and align the
seams.

pouch bottom

2) Sew 1 cm [⅜"] from the
edges to create a flat bottom for
the pouch. Repeat on the
remaining side of the pouch.

3) Sew the gusset of the pouch
lining in the same manner.

5. Finishing the pouch:

1) Attach heavy-duty double-sided tape
to the board for the pouch bottom.

6 cm [2⅜"]
17.5 cm [6⅞"]

3) Blind stitch the opening.

pouch lining (right side)

4) Put the
pouch lining
inside and
smooth out
any wrinkles.

pouch
exterior
(right side)

HOLIDAY

12 cm
[4¾"]

5) Make
and
attach a
tassel.

2) Turn the pouch right side
out. Insert the board into the
lining opening and adhere the
taped side of the board to the
bottom of the pouch exterior.

6 cm [2⅜"]
17.5 cm [6⅞"]

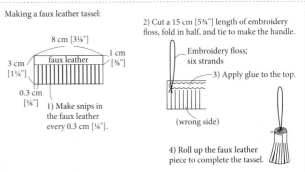

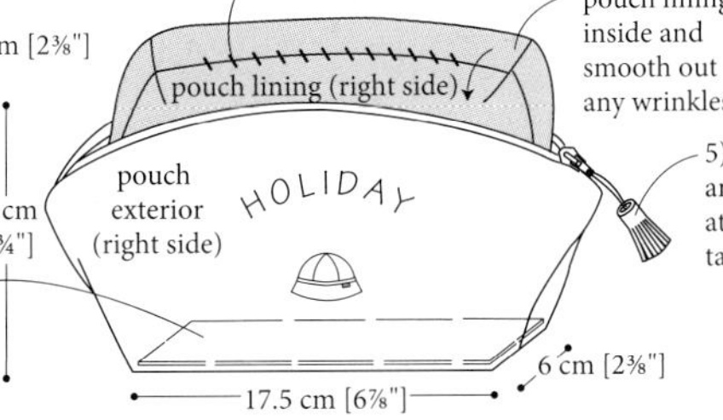

Making a faux leather tassel:

8 cm [3⅛"]

3 cm
[1¼"]

faux leather

1 cm
[⅜"]

0.3 cm
[⅛"]

1) Make snips in
the faux leather
every 0.3 cm [⅛"].

2) Cut a 15 cm [5¾"] length of embroidery
floss, fold in half, and tie to make the handle.

Embroidery floss;
six strands

3) Apply glue to the top.

(wrong side)

4) Roll up the faux leather
piece to complete the tassel.

Summer Vacation

shown on pages 20, 22

• The full-size Summer Vacation embroidery patterns are below.
• The number in the parentheses stands for the number of strands used for the specific stitch.
• See p. 61 for instructions on the outline filling stitch.
• The Olympus embroidery floss number follows each stitch; because Olympus floss is not widely available outside Japan, we have included the DMC floss number in parentheses.

Deck Chair

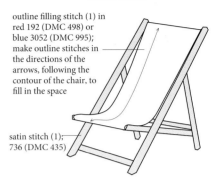

outline filling stitch (1) in red 192 (DMC 498) or blue 3052 (DMC 995); make outline stitches in the directions of the arrows, following the contour of the chair, to fill in the space

satin stitch (1); 736 (DMC 435)

Lighthouse

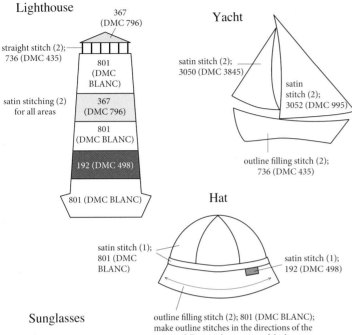

367 (DMC 796)

straight stitch (2); 736 (DMC 435)

801 (DMC BLANC)

satin stitching (2) for all areas

367 (DMC 796)

801 (DMC BLANC)

192 (DMC 498)

801 (DMC BLANC)

Yacht

satin stitch (2); 3050 (DMC 3845)

satin stitch (2); 3052 (DMC 995)

outline filling stitch (2); 736 (DMC 435)

Hat

satin stitch (1); 801 (DMC BLANC)

satin stitch (1); 192 (DMC 498)

outline filling stitch (2); 801 (DMC BLANC); make outline stitches in the directions of the arrows, following the contour of the hat rim, to fill in the space

Sunglasses

split stitch (1); 192 (DMC 498)

satin stitch (1); 900 (DMC 310)

Anchor

buttonhole stitch

Use one strand of embroidery floss 801 (DMC BLANC) for all areas of the anchor.

satin stitch

outline filling stitch; make outline stitches in the directions of the arrows, following the contour of the anchor bottom, to fill in the space

Embroidering the double satin stitch for canvas shoes:

satin stitch (2); 801 (DMC BLANC); start embroidering from the side of the shoes, working vertically

satin stitch (1); 801 (DMC BLANC); start embroidering from the tip of the toes, working horizontally

For the narrow areas of the shoes, backstitch (2); 801 (DMC BLANC) two rows.

* Embroider the borders, using similar-color floss.

Canvas Shoes

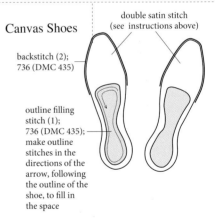

double satin stitch (see instructions above)

backstitch (2); 736 (DMC 435)

outline filling stitch (1); 736 (DMC 435); make outline stitches in the directions of the arrow, following the outline of the shoe, to fill in the space

double satin stitch (see instructions above)

(1); 367 (DMC 796)

(1); 801 (DMC BLANC)

backstitch (2); 736 (DMC 435)

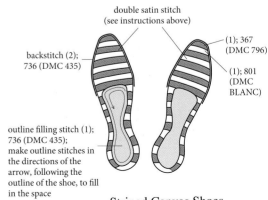

outline filling stitch (1); 736 (DMC 435); make outline stitches in the directions of the arrow, following the outline of the shoe, to fill in the space

Striped Canvas Shoes

Stitch Lesson 8

Embroidering the Split Stitch

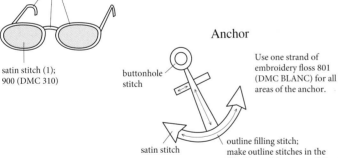

4 in

3 out   1 out   2 in

8 in   6 in   4 in

7 out   5 out   3   1   2

1. The needle comes out from the back at (1), goes down into the fabric at (2), and back out of the fabric at (3). Insert needle at (4), piercing the thread just ahead of (1).

2. Continue stitching, similar to a backstitch, piercing the thread of the previous stitch each time.

Sailor

shown on page 23

- The full-size Sailor embroidery pattern is at right.
- The number in the parentheses stands for the number of strands used for the specific stitch.
- See p. 61 for instructions on the outline filling stitch.
- The Olympus embroidery floss number follows each stitch; because Olympus floss is not widely available outside Japan, we have included the DMC floss number in parentheses.

letters:
outline stitch (2);
two rows 368 (DMC 820)

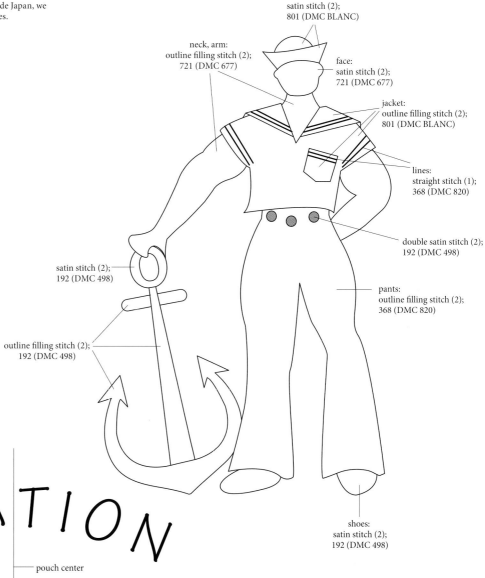

satin stitch (2);
801 (DMC BLANC)

neck, arm:
outline filling stitch (2);
721 (DMC 677)

face:
satin stitch (2);
721 (DMC 677)

jacket:
outline filling stitch (2);
801 (DMC BLANC)

lines:
straight stitch (1);
368 (DMC 820)

double satin stitch (2);
192 (DMC 498)

satin stitch (2);
192 (DMC 498)

pants:
outline filling stitch (2);
368 (DMC 820)

outline filling stitch (2);
192 (DMC 498)

shoes:
satin stitch (2);
192 (DMC 498)

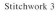

Summer vacation

shown on page 21

- The full-size Vacation embroidery pattern for the Medium Pouch on p. 21 is below.
- The full-size pattern for the Medium Pouch is on p. 53.
- The number in the parentheses stands for the number of strands used for the specific stitch.
- See p. 61 for instructions on the outline filling stitch.
- The Olympus embroidery floss number follows each stitch; because Olympus floss is not widely available outside Japan, we have included the DMC floss number in parentheses.

letters:
outline stitch (2);
two rows 801
(DMC BLANC)

Use two strands of
embroidery floss 366
(DMC 797) for all areas
of anchor.

pouch center

buttonhole stitch

outline filling stitch

satin stitch

outline filling stitch; make outline
stitches in the directions of the
arrows, following the contour of the
anchor bottom, to fill in the space.

Marine de France

shown on page 24

- The full-size Marine de France embroidery patterns are below.
- The number in the parentheses stands for the number of strands used for the specific stitch.
- See p. 61 for instructions on the outline filling stitch.
- The Olympus embroidery floss number follows each stitch; because Olympus floss is not widely available outside Japan, we have included the DMC floss number in parentheses.

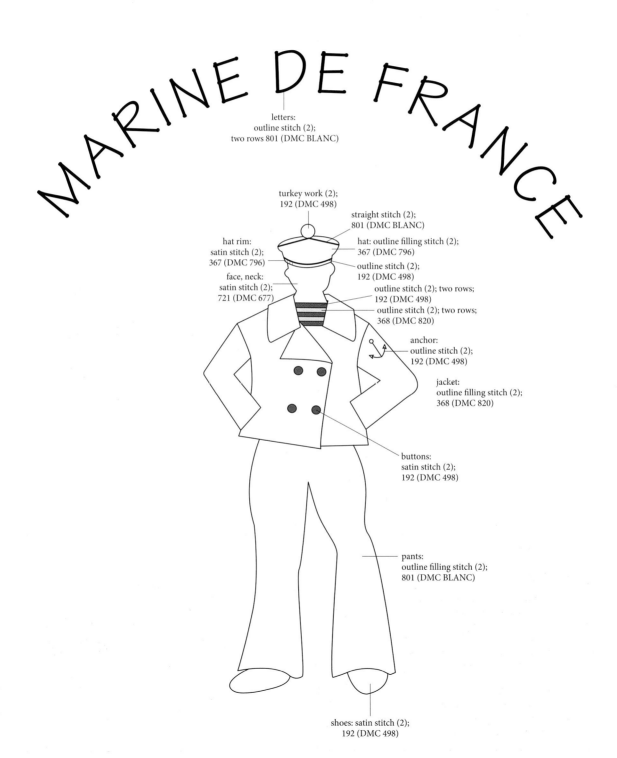

letters:
outline stitch (2);
two rows 801 (DMC BLANC)

turkey work (2);
192 (DMC 498)

straight stitch (2);
801 (DMC BLANC)

hat rim:
satin stitch (2);
367 (DMC 796)

hat: outline filling stitch (2);
367 (DMC 796)

outline stitch (2);
192 (DMC 498)

face, neck:
satin stitch (2);
721 (DMC 677)

outline stitch (2); two rows;
192 (DMC 498)

outline stitch (2); two rows;
368 (DMC 820)

anchor:
outline stitch (2);
192 (DMC 498)

jacket:
outline filling stitch (2);
368 (DMC 820)

buttons:
satin stitch (2);
192 (DMC 498)

pants:
outline filling stitch (2);
801 (DMC BLANC)

shoes: satin stitch (2);
192 (DMC 498)

Porter

shown on page 25

- The full-size Porter embroidery patterns are below.
- The number in the parentheses stands for the number of strands used for the specific stitch.
- See below for instructions on the outline filling stitch.
- The Olympus embroidery floss number follows each stitch; because Olympus floss is not widely available outside Japan, we have included the DMC floss number in parentheses.

letters:
outline stitch (2);
two rows 900 (DMC 310)

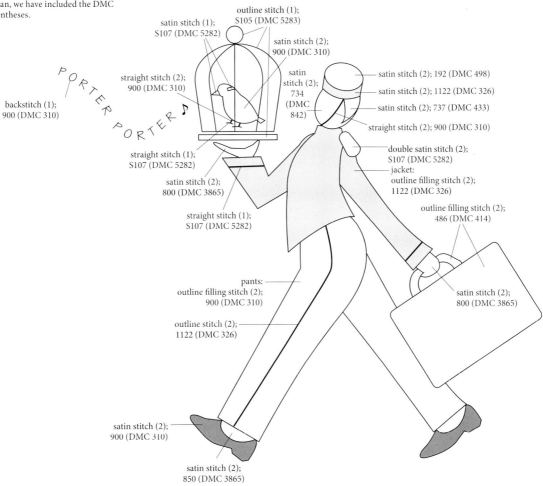

satin stitch (1);
S107 (DMC 5282)

outline stitch (1);
S105 (DMC 5283)

satin stitch (2);
900 (DMC 310)

satin stitch (2);
734 (DMC 842)

straight stitch (2);
900 (DMC 310)

backstitch (1);
900 (DMC 310)

satin stitch (2); 192 (DMC 498)

satin stitch (2); 1122 (DMC 326)

satin stitch (2); 737 (DMC 433)

straight stitch (2); 900 (DMC 310)

double satin stitch (2);
S107 (DMC 5282)

jacket:
outline filling stitch (2);
1122 (DMC 326)

straight stitch (1);
S107 (DMC 5282)

satin stitch (2);
800 (DMC 3865)

outline filling stitch (2);
486 (DMC 414)

straight stitch (1);
S107 (DMC 5282)

pants:
outline filling stitch (2);
900 (DMC 310)

outline stitch (2);
1122 (DMC 326)

satin stitch (2);
800 (DMC 3865)

satin stitch (2);
900 (DMC 310)

satin stitch (2);
850 (DMC 3865)

Stitch Lesson 9

Outline Filling Stitch

In this book, the technique called "outline filling stitch" is often used to fill in large areas. Compared to the satin stitch or short stitch, the outline filling stitch is easier and has a more beautiful finish. Using an outline stitch (see p. 40 for instructions), work from one edge of the space to the other, then work back in the opposite direction, placing rows of stitching right next to each other. When embroidering a curved line or circle, draw guidelines beforehand. Working along these guidelines will result in balanced curves and even stitches. For an extreme curve, try not to forcibly fill in the area. You can always add more stitches later.

When embroidering a circle, use a water-soluble marker to draw guidelines.

guideline

Work stitches back and forth across the space, following the guidelines.

To draw guidelines on a curved area, follow the arrows marked on the embroidery pattern.

guideline

Tote bag

shown on pages **13, 15, 27**

Materials needed

See individual embroidery motifs on pp. 63, 50, and 51 for information on embroidery threads.
Linen (bag exterior, handles), 50 x 50 cm [20" x 20"]
Printed fabric (bag lining), 40 x 50 cm [16" x 20"]
Interfacing, 90 x 50 cm [36" x 20"]
Board for the bottom (thin cardboard or plastic), 22 x 10 cm [8⅝" x 4"]
Heavy-duty double-sided tape

Only for the Violet and Hollyhock bags:
Grosgrain ribbon, two 1.5 x 35 cm (⅝" x 13¾") pieces

1. Embroidering and cutting fabric pieces:

- The full-size bag pattern is on p. 53.
- For embroidery patterns, see individual pages as indicated in the instructions below.

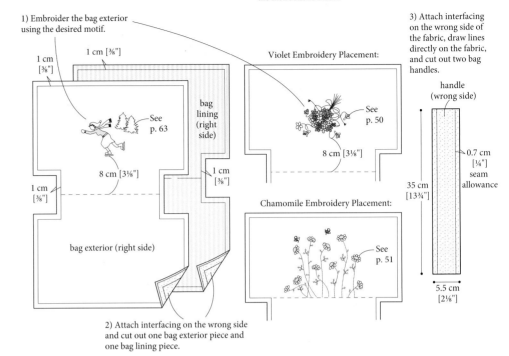

1) Embroider the bag exterior using the desired motif.

1 cm [⅜"]
1 cm [⅜"]

bag lining (right side)

See p. 63

8 cm [3⅛"]

1 cm [⅜"]

1 cm [⅜"]

bag exterior (right side)

Violet Embroidery Placement:

See p. 50

8 cm [3⅛"]

Chamomile Embroidery Placement:

See p. 51

3) Attach interfacing on the wrong side of the fabric, draw lines directly on the fabric, and cut out two bag handles.

handle (wrong side)

0.7 cm [¼"] seam allowance

35 cm [13¾"]

5.5 cm [2⅛"]

2) Attach interfacing on the wrong side and cut out one bag exterior piece and one bag lining piece.

2. Making the bag handles:

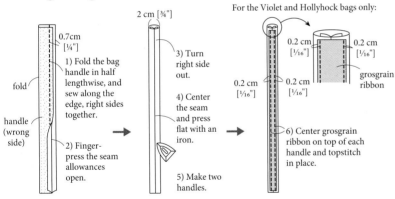

0.7cm [¼"]

1) Fold the bag handle in half lengthwise, and sew along the edge, right sides together.

fold

handle (wrong side)

2) Finger-press the seam allowances open.

2 cm [¾"]

3) Turn right side out.

4) Center the seam and press flat with an iron.

5) Make two handles.

For the Violet and Hollyhock bags only:

0.2 cm [1/16"]
0.2 cm [1/16"]
grosgrain ribbon

0.2 cm [1/16"]
0.2 cm [1/16"]

6) Center grosgrain ribbon on top of each handle and topstitch in place.

3. Basting bag handles in place:

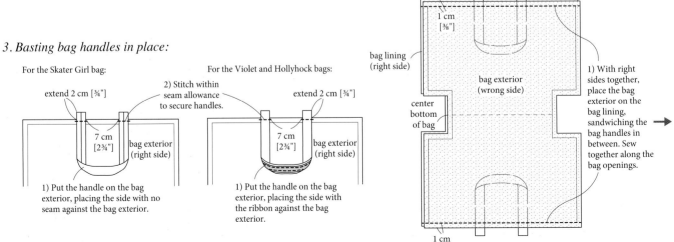

For the Skater Girl bag:

extend 2 cm [¾"]

2) Stitch within seam allowance to secure handles.

7 cm [2¾"]

bag exterior (right side)

1) Put the handle on the bag exterior, placing the side with no seam against the bag exterior.

For the Violet and Hollyhock bags:

extend 2 cm [¾"]

7 cm [2¾"]

bag exterior (right side)

1) Put the handle on the bag exterior, placing the side with the ribbon against the bag exterior.

4. Sewing bag exterior and lining together:

1 cm [⅜"]

bag lining (right side)

bag exterior (wrong side)

center bottom of bag

1) With right sides together, place the bag exterior on the bag lining, sandwiching the bag handles in between. Sew together along the bag openings.

1 cm [⅜"]

Continued on p. 63

Skater Girl

shown on page 26

- The full-size Skater Girl embroidery patterns are below.
- The number in the parentheses stands for the number of strands used for the specific stitch.
- See p. 61 for instructions on the outline filling stitch.
- See p. 74 for how to make modified overcast stitches.
- The Olympus embroidery floss number follows each stitch; because Olympus floss is not widely available outside Japan, we have included the DMC floss number in parentheses.
- Colors listed below are for the colors used on p. 26. To make the colors the same as on the bag on p. 27, use 173 (DMC 946) for the sweater and 192 (DMC 498) for the scarf and hat.

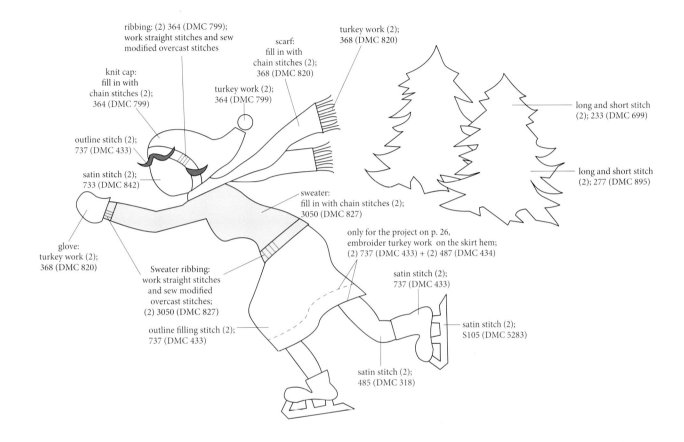

ribbing: (2) 364 (DMC 799); work straight stitches and sew modified overcast stitches

scarf: fill in with chain stitches (2); 368 (DMC 820)

turkey work (2); 368 (DMC 820)

knit cap: fill in with chain stitches (2); 364 (DMC 799)

turkey work (2); 364 (DMC 799)

long and short stitch (2); 233 (DMC 699)

outline stitch (2); 737 (DMC 433)

satin stitch (2); 733 (DMC 842)

long and short stitch (2); 277 (DMC 895)

sweater: fill in with chain stitches (2); 3050 (DMC 827)

only for the project on p. 26, embroider turkey work on the skirt hem; (2) 737 (DMC 433) + (2) 487 (DMC 434)

glove: turkey work (2); 368 (DMC 820)

satin stitch (2); 737 (DMC 433)

Sweater ribbing: work straight stitches and sew modified overcast stitches; (2) 3050 (DMC 827)

satin stitch (2); S105 (DMC 5283)

outline filling stitch (2); 737 (DMC 433)

satin stitch (2); 485 (DMC 318)

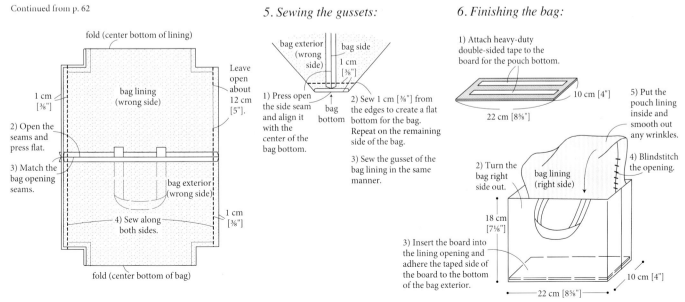

Continued from p. 62

fold (center bottom of lining)

1 cm [⅜"]

2) Open the seams and press flat.

3) Match the bag opening seams.

bag lining (wrong side)

Leave open about 12 cm [5"].

bag exterior (wrong side)

4) Sew along both sides.

1 cm [⅜"]

fold (center bottom of bag)

5. Sewing the gussets:

bag exterior (wrong side)

bag side

1 cm [⅜"]

bag bottom

1) Press open the side seam and align it with the center of the bag bottom.

2) Sew 1 cm [⅜"] from the edges to create a flat bottom for the bag. Repeat on the remaining side of the bag.

3) Sew the gusset of the bag lining in the same manner.

6. Finishing the bag:

1) Attach heavy-duty double-sided tape to the board for the pouch bottom.

10 cm [4"]

22 cm [8⅝"]

5) Put the pouch lining inside and smooth out any wrinkles.

2) Turn the bag right side out.

bag lining (right side)

4) Blindstitch the opening.

18 cm [7⅛"]

3) Insert the board into the lining opening and adhere the taped side of the board to the bottom of the bag exterior.

10 cm [4"]

22 cm [8⅝"]

Petit boxes

shown on pages 8, 9

Embroider on linen and make a petit box.
• See p. 47 for the Favorite Things embroidery motifs.

• See the pages listed below for materials and instructions for each box.
[1. Square petit box] → See p. 69
[2. Rectangular petit box] → See p. 68
[3. Cylinder petit box] → See p. 71
[4. Round petit box] → See p. 50
[5, 6. Oval petit box] → See p. 70

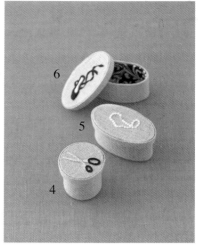

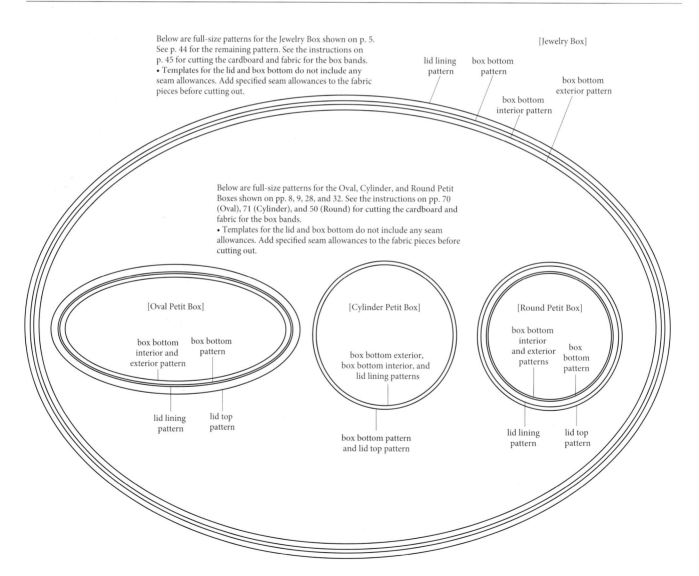

Below are full-size patterns for the Jewelry Box shown on p. 5.
See p. 44 for the remaining pattern. See the instructions on
p. 45 for cutting the cardboard and fabric for the box bands.
• Templates for the lid and box bottom do not include any
seam allowances. Add specified seam allowances to the fabric
pieces before cutting out.

[Jewelry Box]

lid lining pattern

box bottom pattern

box bottom exterior pattern

box bottom interior pattern

Below are full-size patterns for the Oval, Cylinder, and Round Petit
Boxes shown on pp. 8, 9, 28, and 32. See the instructions on pp. 70
(Oval), 71 (Cylinder), and 50 (Round) for cutting the cardboard and
fabric for the box bands.
• Templates for the lid and box bottom do not include any seam
allowances. Add specified seam allowances to the fabric pieces before
cutting out.

[Oval Petit Box]

box bottom interior and exterior pattern

box bottom pattern

lid lining pattern

lid top pattern

[Cylinder Petit Box]

box bottom exterior, box bottom interior, and lid lining patterns

box bottom pattern and lid top pattern

[Round Petit Box]

box bottom interior and exterior patterns

box bottom pattern

lid lining pattern

lid top pattern

Monograms

shown on pages 28, 29

Choose a letter from the sampler and embroider it on linen to make a petit box (see the alphabet sampler below for embroidery motifs).

• See the pages listed below for materials and instructions for each box.
[1, 2. Square petit box] → See p. 69
[3, 4. Cylinder petit box] → See p. 71
[5. Rectangular petit box] → See p. 68

• To make the dot embroidered between letters E and O on box 5 in the picture, work the French knot stitch (2), wrap two times.
• The number in the parentheses stands for the number of strands used for the specific stitch.
• See p. 61 for instructions on the outline filling stitch.
• All monograms were stitched in Olympus embroidery floss 192 (DMC 498).

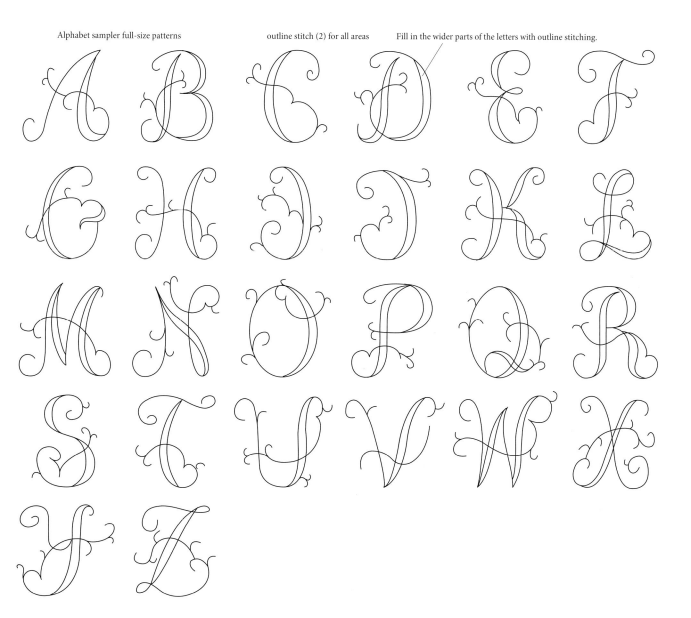

Alphabet sampler full-size patterns   outline stitch (2) for all areas   Fill in the wider parts of the letters with outline stitching.

Snowflake petit boxes

shown on page 32

Embroider on linen and make a petit box.
• The full-size Snowflake embroidery patterns are below.
• See the pages listed below for materials and instructions for each box.
[1, 2. Rectangular petit box] → See p. 68
[3, 4. Cylinder petit box] → See p. 71
[5. Oval petit box] → See p. 70
[6. Square petit box] → See p. 69

• The Olympus embroidery floss number is listed for each box; because Olympus floss is not widely
available outside Japan, we have included the DMC floss number in parentheses.

[1. Rectangular petit box]
• Use three strands S105 (DMC 5283) for all areas.

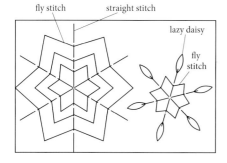

[2. Rectangular petit box]
• Use three strands 801 (DMC BLANC) for all areas.

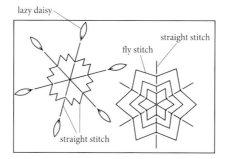

[3. Cylinder petit box]
• Use three strands 801 (DMC BLANC) for all areas.

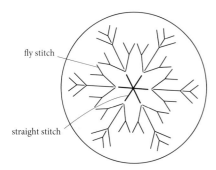

[4. Cylinder petit box]
• Use two strands S105 (DMC 5283) for all areas.

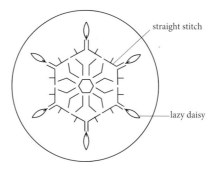

[5. Oval petit box]
• Use three strands 801 (DMC BLANC) for all areas.

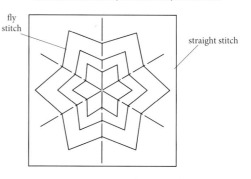

[6. Square petit box]
• Use three strands 801 (DMC BLANC) for all areas.

Monogram box

shown on page **29**

Materials needed

Linen (lid, box band, hinge), 50 x 20 cm [20" x 8"]
Printed fabric (lid lining, inner box, box bottom interior),
    50 x 15 cm [20" x 6"]
Cardboard
    (2 mm), 40 x 20 cm [16" x 8"];
    (0.5 mm), 25 x 20 cm [10" x 8"]
Cotton tape, 0.5 cm x 50cm [¼" x 19¾"]
White craft glue
Embroidery floss: red

- The full-size Monogram Box embroidery patterns are below.
- Use two strands 1122 (DMC 326) for all areas.
- See p. 61 for instructions on the outline filling stitch.
- See p. 72 for instructions for the rectangle box.

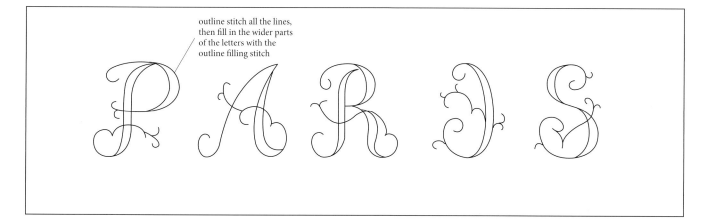

outline stitch all the lines, then fill in the wider parts of the letters with the outline filling stitch

Snowflake box

shown on page **33**

Materials needed

Linen (lid, box band, hinge), 50 x 20 cm [20" x 8"]
Printed fabric (lid lining, inner box, box bottom
    interior), 50 x 15 cm [20" x 6"]
Cardboard
    (2 mm), 40 x 20 cm [16" x 8"];
    (0.5 mm), 25 x 20 cm [10" x 8"]
Rhinestones (5 mm) 3 pcs; (4 mm) 5 pcs; (3 mm) 5 pcs
Embroidery floss: white
White craft glue

- The full-size Snowflake Box embroidery patterns are below.
- Use 801 (DMC BLANC) for all areas of stitching.
- See p. 72 for instructions for the rectangle box.
- The number in the parentheses stands for the number of strands used for the specific stitch.

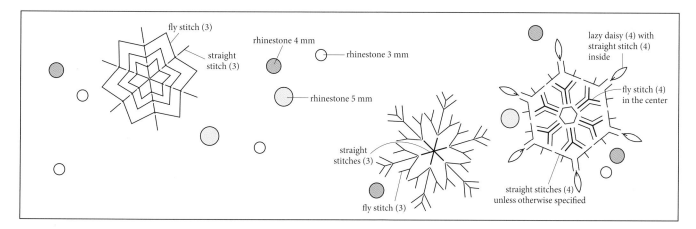

fly stitch (3)

straight stitch (3)

rhinestone 4 mm

rhinestone 3 mm

rhinestone 5 mm

lazy daisy (4) with straight stitch (4) inside

fly stitch (4) in the center

straight stitches (3)

fly stitch (3)

straight stitches (4) unless otherwise specified

Rectangular petit box

shown on pages 8, 28, 32

Materials needed

See individual embroidery motifs for information on embroidery threads
Linen (lid, box band, box bottom exterior), 30 x 10 cm [12" x 4"]
Printed fabric (lid lining, inner box), 20 x 10 cm [8" x 4"]
Cardboard
(1 mm), 25 x 10 cm [10" x 4"];
(0.5 mm), 15 x 10 cm [6" x 4"]
White craft glue

1. Cutting cardboard pieces:

• Using the measurements shown below, draw lines on the cardboard and cut out one of each piece.

1) Cut away all the areas marked with diagonal lines.

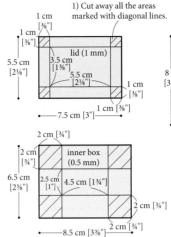

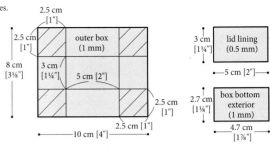

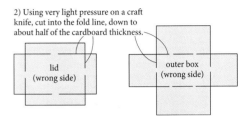

2) Using very light pressure on a craft knife, cut into the fold line, down to about half of the cardboard thickness.

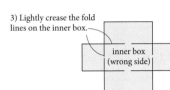

3) Lightly crease the fold lines on the inner box.

2. Cutting fabric pieces:

• Using the measurements shown below, draw lines on the fabric and cut one of each piece.

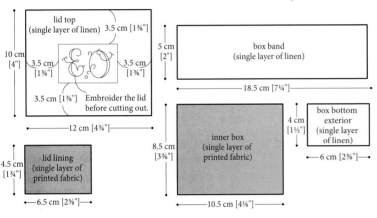

Embroider the lid before cutting out.

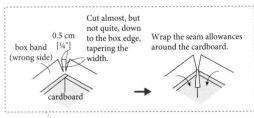

Cut almost, but not quite, down to the box edge, tapering the width.

0.5 cm [¼"]

box band (wrong side)

Wrap the seam allowances around the cardboard.

cardboard

3. Making the outer box and lid:

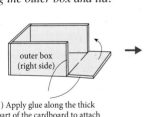

outer box (right side)

1) Apply glue along the thick part of the cardboard to attach sides and make a box.

2) Apply glue to the cardboard, then wrap the fabric around the box.

1 cm [⅜"]

1.5 cm [⅝"]

box band (wrong side)

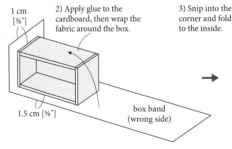

3) Snip into the corner and fold over to the inside.

Fold down the edge and overlap.

4) Fold the fabric over to the box bottom and press in place.

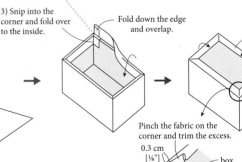

Pinch the fabric on the corner and trim the excess.

0.3 cm [⅛"]

box bottom

5) Assemble the lid in the same manner as the box.

4. Making and adding the box bottom exterior:

1) Apply glue to the cardboard, center it on the fabric, and press in place.

0.3 cm [⅛"]

2) Snip along the corner.

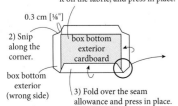

box bottom exterior cardboard

box bottom exterior (wrong side)

3) Fold over the seam allowance and press in place.

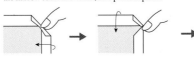

Press down the corner with your fingernail, fold over the narrow seam allowance, and press in place.

4) Glue the box bottom exterior to the outside box.

box bottom exterior (right side)

box band (right side)

5. Making and adding the inner box:

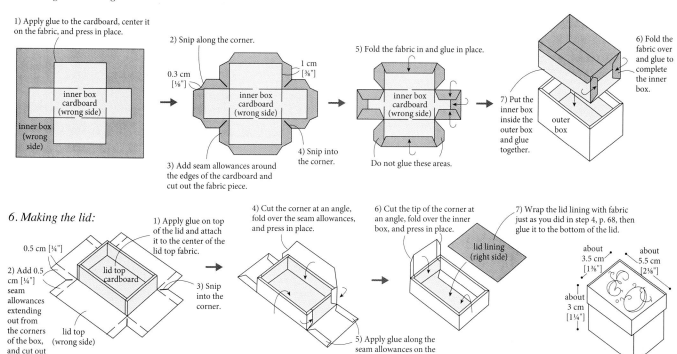

1) Apply glue to the cardboard, center it on the fabric, and press in place.

inner box cardboard (wrong side)

inner box (wrong side)

2) Snip along the corner.

0.3 cm [⅛"]

1 cm [⅜"]

inner box cardboard (wrong side)

3) Add seam allowances around the edges of the cardboard and cut out the fabric piece.

4) Snip into the corner.

5) Fold the fabric in and glue in place.

inner box cardboard (wrong side)

Do not glue these areas.

6) Fold the fabric over and glue to complete the inner box.

7) Put the inner box inside the outer box and glue together.

outer box

6. Making the lid:

1) Apply glue on top of the lid and attach it to the center of the lid top fabric.

0.5 cm [¼"]

2) Add 0.5 cm [¼"] seam allowances extending out from the corners of the box, and cut out the fabric piece.

lid top cardboard

3) Snip into the corner.

lid top (wrong side)

4) Cut the corner at an angle, fold over the seam allowances, and press in place.

5) Apply glue along the seam allowances on the short end and fold in.

6) Cut the tip of the corner at an angle, fold over the inner box, and press in place.

7) Wrap the lid lining with fabric just as you did in step 4, p. 68, then glue it to the bottom of the lid.

lid lining (right side)

about 3.5 cm [1⅜"]

about 5.5 cm [2⅛"]

about 3 cm [1¼"]

Square petit box

shown on pages 8, 28, 32

Materials needed

See individual embroidery motifs for information on embroidery threads.
Linen (lid, box band, box bottom exterior), 30 x 15 cm [12" x 6"]
Printed fabric (lid lining, inner box), 20 x 15 cm [8" x 6"]
Cardboard
 (1 mm), 20 x 15 cm [8" x 6"];
 (0.5 mm), 15 x 10 cm [6" x 4"]
White craft glue

1. Cutting cardboard pieces:

• Using the measurements shown below, draw lines on the cardboard and cut out one of each piece.

1) Cut away all the areas marked with diagonal lines.

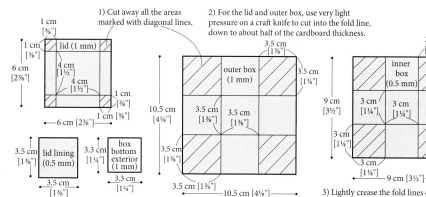

1 cm [⅜"]

1 cm [⅜"]

lid (1 mm)

4 cm [1½"]

4 cm [1½"]

6 cm [2⅜"]

1 cm [⅜"]

1 cm [⅜"]

6 cm [2⅜"]

3.5 cm [1⅜"]
lid lining (0.5 mm)
3.5 cm [1⅜"]

3.3 cm [1¼"]
box bottom exterior (1 mm)
3.3 cm [1¼"]

2) For the lid and outer box, use very light pressure on a craft knife to cut into the fold line, down to about half of the cardboard thickness.

3.5 cm [1⅜"]

outer box (1 mm)

3.5 cm [1⅜"]

3.5 cm [1⅜"]

3.5 cm [1⅜"]

10.5 cm [4⅛"]

3.5 cm [1⅜"]

3.5 cm [1⅜"]   10.5 cm [4⅛"]

3 cm [1¼"]

inner box (0.5 mm)

3 cm [1¼"]

3 cm [1¼"]

9 cm [3½"]

3 cm [1¼"]

3 cm [1¼"]

3 cm [1¼"]

9 cm [3½"]

3) Lightly crease the fold lines on the inner box. (See step 1 of the instructions for the rectangular petit box on p. 68.)

2. Cutting fabric pieces:

• Using the measurements shown below, draw lines on the fabric and cut one of each piece.

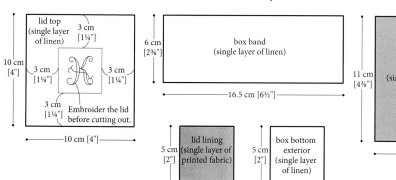

lid top (single layer of linen)

3 cm [1¼"]

10 cm [4"]

3 cm [1¼"]

K

3 cm [1¼"]

3 cm [1¼"]

Embroider the lid before cutting out.

10 cm [4"]

6 cm [2⅜"]

box band (single layer of linen)

16.5 cm [6½"]

5 cm [2"]
lid lining (single layer of printed fabric)
5 cm [2"]

5 cm [2"]
box bottom exterior (single layer of linen)
5 cm [2"]

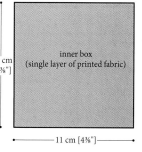

11 cm [4⅜"]

inner box (single layer of printed fabric)

11 cm [4⅜"]

3. Repeat steps 3 through 6 of instructions for the Rectangular Petit Box on pp. 68 and 69 to finish the box.

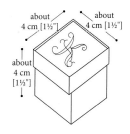

about 4 cm [1½"]

about 4 cm [1½"]

about 4 cm [1½"]

Oval petit box

shown on pages **9, 28, 32**

1. Cutting cardboard pieces:

- The full-size patterns are on p. 64.
- Cut one of each piece.
- Using the measurements shown below, draw lines on the cardboard and cut out box band and lid band pieces.

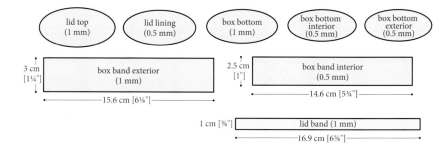

Materials needed

See individual embroidery motifs for information on embroidery threads
Linen (lid top, lid band, box band exterior, box bottom exterior), 30 x 10 cm [12" x 4"]
Printed fabric (lid lining, box band interior, box bottom interior), 20 x 10 cm [8" x 4"]
Cardboard
  (1 mm), 20 x 10 cm [8" x 4"];
  (0.5 mm), 15 x 10 cm [6" x 4"]
White craft glue

lid top (1 mm) | lid lining (0.5 mm) | box bottom (1 mm) | box bottom interior (0.5 mm) | box bottom exterior (0.5 mm)

3 cm [1¼"] — box band exterior (1 mm) — 15.6 cm [6⅛"]

2.5 cm [1"] — box band interior (0.5 mm) — 14.6 cm [5¾"]

1 cm [⅜"] — lid band (1 mm) — 16.9 cm [6⅝"]

2. Cutting fabric pieces:

- Add seam allowances as shown to the lid top, lid lining, box bottom exterior, and box bottom interior patterns and cut out.
- Cut one of each fabric piece.
- Using the measurements shown below, draw lines on the fabric and cut out the box band pieces.

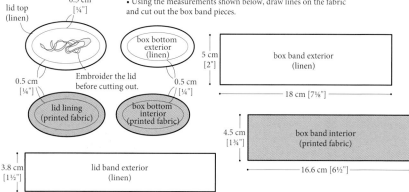

lid top (linen)
0.5 cm [¼"]
0.5 cm [¼"]
Embroider the lid before cutting out.

box bottom exterior (linen)
0.5 cm [¼"]

lid lining (printed fabric)

box bottom interior (printed fabric)

box band exterior (linen)
5 cm [2"]
18 cm [7⅛"]

box band interior (printed fabric)
4.5 cm [1¾"]
16.6 cm [6½"]

lid band exterior (linen)
3.8 cm [1½"]
19.5 cm [7⅝"]

3. Assembling cardboard pieces:

1) Apply glue on the ends of the box band exterior, lay the ends flush against each other, and glue in place.

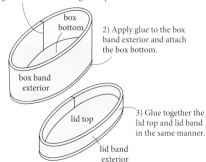

2) Apply glue to the box band exterior and attach the box bottom.

box bottom

box band exterior

3) Glue together the lid top and lid band in the same manner.

lid top

lid band exterior

4. Gluing the box band exterior and box bottom interior to the box:

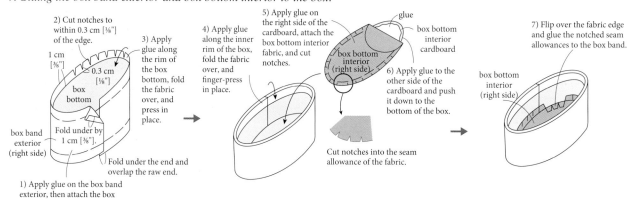

2) Cut notches to within 0.3 cm [⅛"] of the edge.

1 cm [⅜"]
0.3 cm [⅛"]

3) Apply glue along the rim of the box bottom, fold the fabric over, and press in place.

box bottom

box band exterior (right side)

Fold under by 1 cm [⅜"].

Fold under the end and overlap the raw end.

1) Apply glue on the box band exterior, then attach the box band exterior fabric.

4) Apply glue along the inner rim of the box, fold the fabric over, and finger-press in place.

5) Apply glue on the right side of the cardboard, attach the box bottom interior fabric, and cut notches.

glue

box bottom interior cardboard

box bottom interior (right side)

6) Apply glue to the other side of the cardboard and push it down to the bottom of the box.

Cut notches into the seam allowance of the fabric.

7) Flip over the fabric edge and glue the notched seam allowances to the box band.

box bottom interior (right side)

5. Making and adding the box band interior and box bottom exterior:

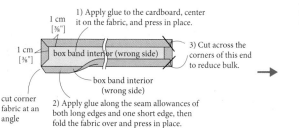

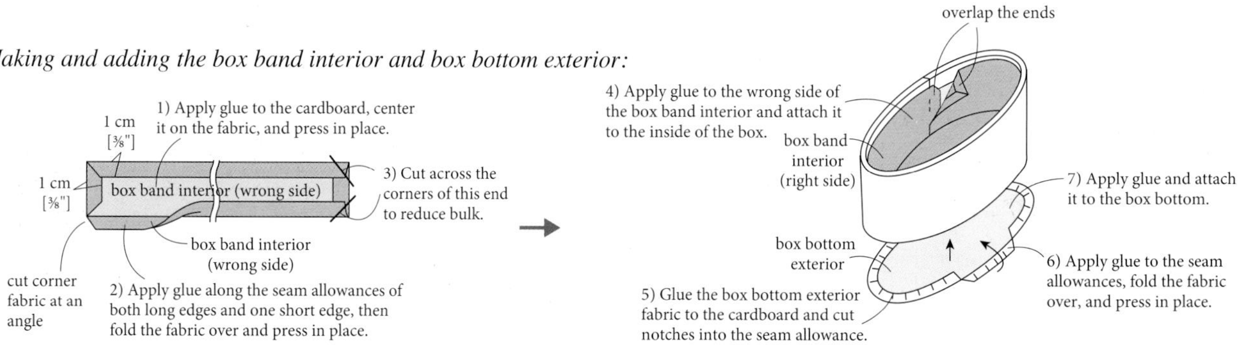

1) Apply glue to the cardboard, center it on the fabric, and press in place.

1 cm [⅜"]
1 cm [⅜"]

box band interior (wrong side)

3) Cut across the corners of this end to reduce bulk.

cut corner fabric at an angle

box band interior (wrong side)

2) Apply glue along the seam allowances of both long edges and one short edge, then fold the fabric over and press in place.

4) Apply glue to the wrong side of the box band interior and attach it to the inside of the box.

overlap the ends

box band interior (right side)

box bottom exterior

7) Apply glue and attach it to the box bottom.

6) Apply glue to the seam allowances, fold the fabric over, and press in place.

5) Glue the box bottom exterior fabric to the cardboard and cut notches into the seam allowance.

6. Making the lid:

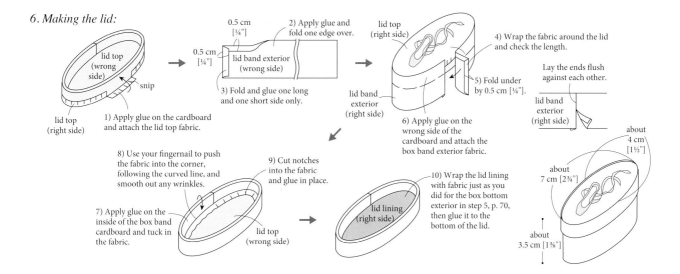

1) Apply glue on the cardboard and attach the lid top fabric.

lid top (wrong side)

lid top (right side)

snip

0.5 cm [¼"]

0.5 cm [¼"]

lid band exterior (wrong side)

2) Apply glue and fold one edge over.

3) Fold and glue one long and one short side only.

lid top (right side)

4) Wrap the fabric around the lid and check the length.

5) Fold under by 0.5 cm [¼"].

lid band exterior (right side)

6) Apply glue on the wrong side of the cardboard and attach the box band exterior fabric.

Lay the ends flush against each other.

lid band exterior (right side)

about 4 cm [1½"]

about 7 cm [2¾"]

about 3.5 cm [1⅜"]

8) Use your fingernail to push the fabric into the corner, following the curved line, and smooth out any wrinkles.

7) Apply glue on the inside of the box band cardboard and tuck in the fabric.

9) Cut notches into the fabric and glue in place.

lid top (wrong side)

lid lining (right side)

10) Wrap the lid lining with fabric just as you did for the box bottom exterior in step 5, p. 70, then glue it to the bottom of the lid.

Cylinder petit box

shown on pages 8, 28, 32

Materials needed

See individual embroidery motifs for information on embroidery threads.
Linen (lid top, lid band, box band exterior, box bottom exterior), 25 x 10 cm [10" x 4"]
Printed fabric (lid lining, box band interior, box bottom interior), 15 x 10 cm [6" x 4"]
Cardboard
(1 mm), 15 x 10 cm [6" x 4"];
(0.5 mm), 15 x 10 cm [6" x 4"]
White craft glue

3. Assembling the box and adding box band exterior and box bottom interior:

Repeat steps 3 and 4 of instructions for the Oval Petit Box on p. 70.

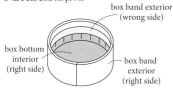

box band exterior (wrong side)

box bottom interior (right side)

box band exterior (right side)

1. Cutting cardboard pieces:

• The full-size patterns are on p. 64.
• Cut one of each piece.
• Using the measurements shown below, draw lines on the cardboard and cut out the box band pieces.

lid top (1 mm)

box bottom (1 mm)

lid lining (0.5 mm)

box bottom interior (0.5 mm)

box bottom exterior (0.5 mm)

1.5 cm [⅝"]   box band exterior (1 mm)   13 cm [5⅛"]

1.5 cm [⅝"]   lid band (1 mm)   13 cm [5⅛"]

2 cm [¾"]   box band interior (0.5 mm)   13 cm [5⅛"]

2. Cutting fabric pieces:

• Add seam allowances as shown to the lid and box bottom patterns and cut out.
• Cut one of each fabric piece.
• Using the measurements shown below, draw lines on the fabric and cut out the box band pieces.

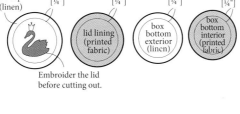

lid top (linen)

0.5 cm [¼"]

lid lining (printed fabric)

box bottom exterior (linen)

box bottom interior (printed fabric)

Embroider the lid before cutting out.

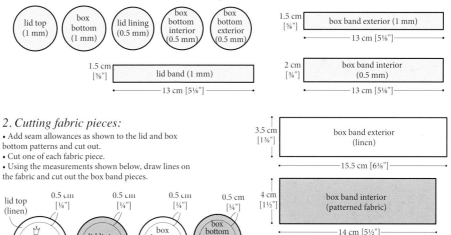

3.5 cm [1⅜"]   box band exterior (linen)   15.5 cm [6⅛"]

4 cm [1½"]   box band interior (patterned fabric)   14 cm [5½"]

5 cm [2"]   lid band exterior (linen)   15.5 cm [6⅛"]

4. Making and adding the box band interior and box bottom exterior:

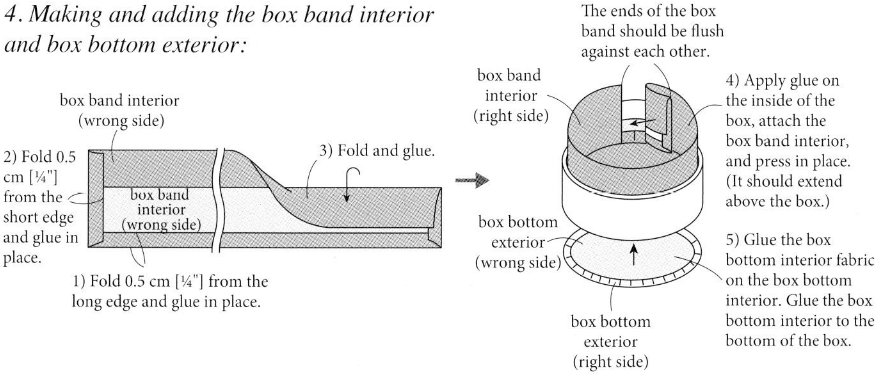

box band interior (wrong side)

2) Fold 0.5 cm [¼"] from the short edge and glue in place.

box band interior (wrong side)

3) Fold and glue.

1) Fold 0.5 cm [¼"] from the long edge and glue in place.

box band interior (right side)

The ends of the box band should be flush against each other.

4) Apply glue on the inside of the box, attach the box band interior, and press in place. (It should extend above the box.)

box bottom exterior (wrong side)

box bottom exterior (right side)

5) Glue the box bottom interior fabric on the box bottom interior. Glue the box bottom interior to the bottom of the box.

5. Making the lid:

Repeat step 6 of instructions for the Oval Petit Box above.

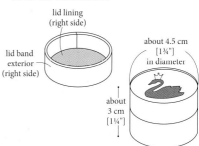

lid lining (right side)

lid band exterior (right side)

about 4.5 cm [1¾"] in diameter

about 3 cm [1¼"]

Rectangle box

shown on pages 29, 33

1. Cutting cardboard pieces:

Using the measurements shown below, draw lines on the cardboard and cut out one or two of each piece as specified.

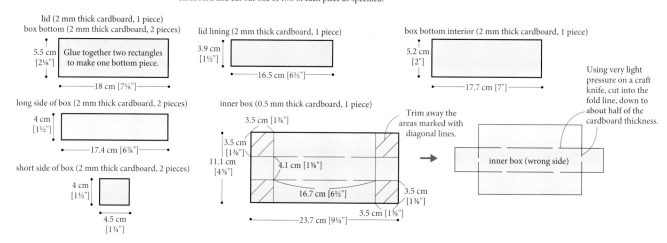

lid (2 mm thick cardboard, 1 piece)
box bottom (2 mm thick cardboard, 2 pieces)

5.5 cm [2⅛"]   Glue together two rectangles to make one bottom piece.

18 cm [7⅛"]

lid lining (2 mm thick cardboard, 1 piece)

3.9 cm [1½"]

16.5 cm [6½"]

box bottom interior (2 mm thick cardboard, 1 piece)

5.2 cm [2"]

17.7 cm [7"]

Using very light pressure on a craft knife, cut into the fold line, down to about half of the cardboard thickness.

long side of box (2 mm thick cardboard, 2 pieces)

4 cm [1½"]

17.4 cm [6⅞"]

short side of box (2 mm thick cardboard, 2 pieces)

4 cm [1½"]

4.5 cm [1¾"]

inner box (0.5 mm thick cardboard, 1 piece)

3.5 cm [1⅜"]

3.5 cm [1⅜"]

11.1 cm [4⅜"]

4.1 cm [1⅝"]

16.7 cm [6½"]

3.5 cm [1⅜"]

3.5 cm [1⅜"]

23.7 cm [9¼"]

Trim away the areas marked with diagonal lines.

inner box (wrong side)

2. Cutting fabric pieces:

• Using the measurements shown below, draw lines on the fabric and cut out the fabric pieces.

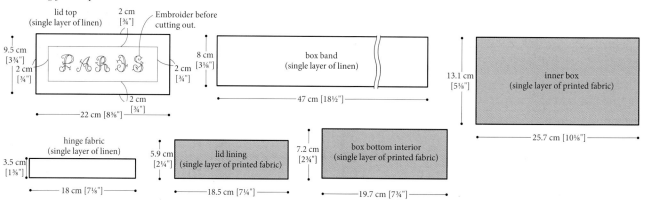

lid top (single layer of linen)

2 cm [¾"]

Embroider before cutting out.

9.5 cm [3¾"]

2 cm [¾"]

P A R I S

2 cm [¾"]

2 cm [¾"]

22 cm [8⅝"]

box band (single layer of linen)

8 cm [3⅛"]

47 cm [18½"]

inner box (single layer of printed fabric)

13.1 cm [5⅛"]

25.7 cm [10⅛"]

hinge fabric (single layer of linen)

3.5 cm [1⅜"]

18 cm [7⅛"]

lid lining (single layer of printed fabric)

5.9 cm [2¼"]

18.5 cm [7¼"]

box bottom interior (single layer of printed fabric)

7.2 cm [2¾"]

19.7 cm [7¾"]

3. Making the outer box:

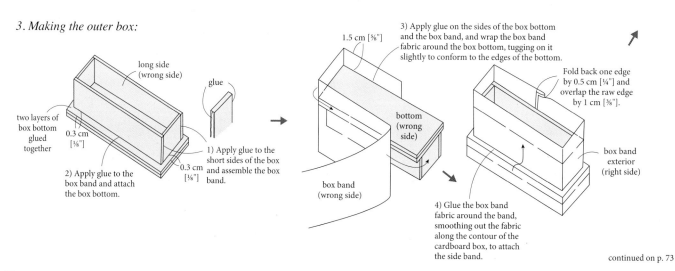

long side (wrong side)

glue

two layers of box bottom glued together

0.3 cm [⅛"]

0.3 cm [⅛"]

1) Apply glue to the short sides of the box and assemble the box band.

2) Apply glue to the box band and attach the box bottom.

1.5 cm [⅝"]

3) Apply glue on the sides of the box bottom and the box band, and wrap the box band fabric around the box bottom, tugging on it slightly to conform to the edges of the bottom.

bottom (wrong side)

box band (wrong side)

4) Glue the box band fabric around the band, smoothing out the fabric along the contour of the cardboard box, to attach the side band.

Fold back one edge by 0.5 cm [¼"] and overlap the raw edge by 1 cm [⅜"].

box band exterior (right side)

continued on p. 73

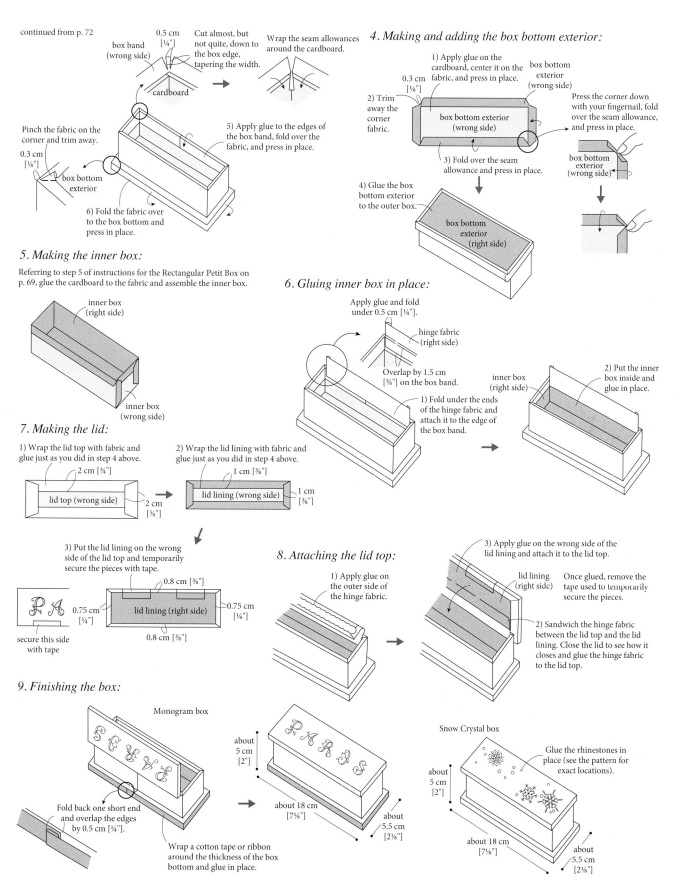

continued from p. 72

box band (wrong side)

0.5 cm [¼"]

Cut almost, but not quite, down to the box edge, tapering the width.

Wrap the seam allowances around the cardboard.

cardboard

4. Making and adding the box bottom exterior:

1) Apply glue on the cardboard, center it on the fabric, and press in place.

box bottom exterior (wrong side)

0.3 cm [⅛"]

2) Trim away the corner fabric.

box bottom exterior (wrong side)

Press the corner down with your fingernail, fold over the seam allowance, and press in place.

box bottom exterior (wrong side)

3) Fold over the seam allowance and press in place.

Pinch the fabric on the corner and trim away.

0.3 cm [⅛"]

box bottom exterior

5) Apply glue to the edges of the box band, fold over the fabric, and press in place.

6) Fold the fabric over to the box bottom and press in place.

4) Glue the box bottom exterior to the outer box.

box bottom exterior (right side)

box bottom exterior (wrong side)

5. Making the inner box:

Referring to step 5 of instructions for the Rectangular Petit Box on p. 69, glue the cardboard to the fabric and assemble the inner box.

inner box (right side)

inner box (wrong side)

6. Gluing inner box in place:

Apply glue and fold under 0.5 cm [¼"].

hinge fabric (right side)

Overlap by 1.5 cm [⅝"] on the box band.

inner box (right side)

2) Put the inner box inside and glue in place.

1) Fold under the ends of the hinge fabric and attach it to the edge of the box band.

7. Making the lid:

1) Wrap the lid top with fabric and glue just as you did in step 4 above.

2 cm [¾"]

lid top (wrong side)

2 cm [¾"]

2) Wrap the lid lining with fabric and glue just as you did in step 4 above.

1 cm [⅜"]

lid lining (wrong side)

1 cm [⅜"]

3) Put the lid lining on the wrong side of the lid top and temporarily secure the pieces with tape.

0.8 cm [⅜"]

0.75 cm [¼"]

lid lining (right side)

0.75 cm [¼"]

0.8 cm [⅜"]

secure this side with tape

8. Attaching the lid top:

1) Apply glue on the outer side of the hinge fabric.

3) Apply glue on the wrong side of the lid lining and attach it to the lid top.

lid lining (right side)

Once glued, remove the tape used to temporarily secure the pieces.

2) Sandwich the hinge fabric between the lid top and the lid lining. Close the lid to see how it closes and glue the hinge fabric to the lid top.

9. Finishing the box:

Monogram box

Fold back one short end and overlap the edges by 0.5 cm [¼"].

Wrap a cotton tape or ribbon around the thickness of the box bottom and glue in place.

about 5 cm [2"]

about 18 cm [7⅛"]

about 5.5 cm [2⅛"]

Snow Crystal box

Glue the rhinestones in place (see the pattern for exact locations).

about 5 cm [2"]

about 18 cm [7⅛"]

about 5.5 cm [2⅛"]

Christmas wreath

shown on page **30**

- The full-size Christmas Wreath embroidery pattern is below.
- The number in the parentheses stands for the number of strands used for the specific stitch.
- The Olympus embroidery floss number follows each stitch; because Olympus floss is not widely available outside Japan, we have included the DMC floss number in parentheses.

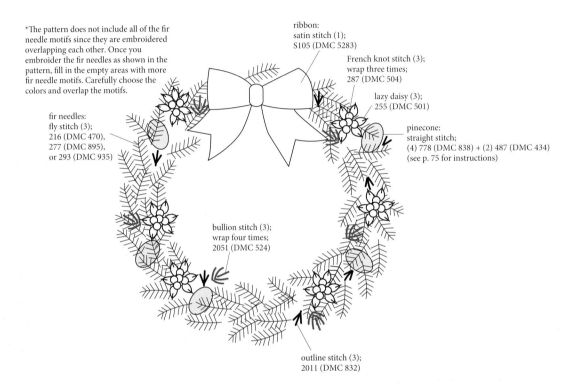

*The pattern does not include all of the fir needle motifs since they are embroidered overlapping each other. Once you embroider the fir needles as shown in the pattern, fill in the empty areas with more fir needle motifs. Carefully choose the colors and overlap the motifs.

ribbon:
satin stitch (1);
S105 (DMC 5283)

French knot stitch (3);
wrap three times;
287 (DMC 504)

lazy daisy (3);
255 (DMC 501)

pinecone:
straight stitch;
(4) 778 (DMC 838) + (2) 487 (DMC 434)
(see p. 75 for instructions)

fir needles:
fly stitch (3);
216 (DMC 470),
277 (DMC 895),
or 293 (DMC 935)

bullion stitch (3);
wrap four times;
2051 (DMC 524)

outline stitch (3);
2011 (DMC 832)

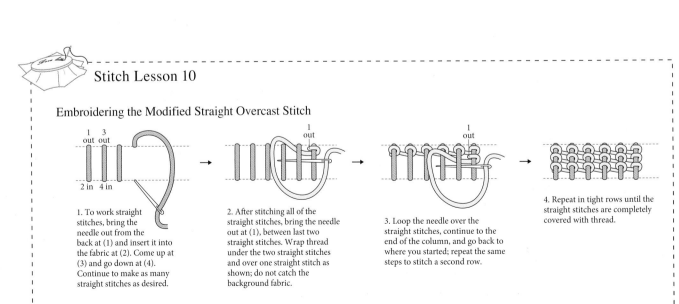

Stitch Lesson 10

Embroidering the Modified Straight Overcast Stitch

1. To work straight stitches, bring the needle out from the back at (1) and insert it into the fabric at (2). Come up at (3) and go down at (4). Continue to make as many straight stitches as desired.

2. After stitching all of the straight stitches, bring the needle out at (1), between last two straight stitches. Wrap thread under the two straight stitches and over one straight stitch as shown; do not catch the background fabric.

3. Loop the needle over the straight stitches, continue to the end of the column, and go back to where you started; repeat the same steps to stitch a second row.

4. Repeat in tight rows until the straight stitches are completely covered with thread.

Christmas tree

shown on page 31

- The full-size Christmas Tree embroidery patterns are below.
- The number in the parentheses stands for the number of strands used for the specific stitch.
- The Olympus embroidery floss number follows each stitch; because Olympus floss is not widely available outside Japan, we have included the DMC floss number in parentheses.

fir tree: fly stitch (2)
Start from the bottom using dark green floss 293 (DMC 935). At the top, use light green floss 216 (DMC 470). In between, use a combination of greens: two strands of dark green floss 293 (DMC 935) and one strand of light green floss 216 (DMC 470) nearer the bottom, and two strands of light green floss 216 (DMC 470) and one strand of dark green floss 293 (DMC 935) nearer the top.

letters:
work backstitches (2);
S105 (DMC 5283);
then overcast stitch (1);
S105 (DMC 5283)

pine cone:
straight stitch;
(4) 737 (DMC 433) +
(2) 487 (DMC 434)

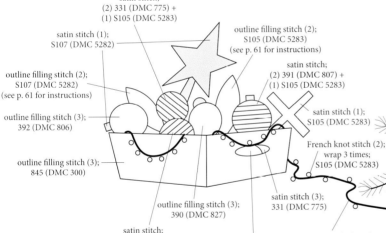

satin stitch;
(2) 331 (DMC 775) +
(1) S105 (DMC 5283)

satin stitch (1);
S107 (DMC 5282)

outline filling stitch (2);
S105 (DMC 5283)
(see p. 61 for instructions)

satin stitch;
(2) 391 (DMC 807) +
(1) S105 (DMC 5283)

outline filling stitch (2);
S107 (DMC 5282)
(see p. 61 for instructions)

satin stitch (1);
S105 (DMC 5283)

outline filling stitch (3);
392 (DMC 806)

French knot stitch (2);
wrap 3 times;
S105 (DMC 5283)

outline filling stitch (3);
845 (DMC 300)

outline filling stitch (3);
390 (DMC 827)

satin stitch (3);
331 (DMC 775)

satin stitch;
(2) 390 (DMC 827) +
(1) S105 (DMC 5283)

satin stitch (3);
391 (DMC 807)

Make a hole at the end of where the cord should be, then bring the ends of 1 mm wide silver cord to the back of the fabric. Thread two strands of matching embroidery floss S105 (DMC 5283) and secure the cord with couching stitches.

Stitch Lesson 11

Embroidering a Pinecone

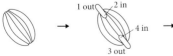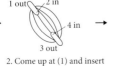

1 out   2 in
4 in
3 out

1. To increase the roundness and depth of the pinecone, first make five to six stitches originating and ending at the same point.

2. Come up at (1) and insert the needle back into the fabric at (2) to make a straight stitch at the tip of the stitches. Repeat to make a stitch at the bottom.

3. Starting from the top, work from outside to the center to make more straight stitches.

4. Don't worry about precision—an uneven contour makes your work look more like a pinecone.

Delineating the fir branches:
Make small straight stitches (2); 737 (DMC 433); at the center of the fir needle.

fly stitch (2)

Make a small straight stitch; (2) 737 (DMC 433); to tie down the loop.

Bundle Up

shown on page 34

Materials needed

Linen (background fabric), as needed
Felt (right front, left front, right sleeve, left
  sleeve, collar), 15 x 15 cm [6" x 6"]
Silk (back, right back), 10 x 15 cm [4" x 6"]
Embroidery floss: black
Glitter embroidery floss: gold

1. Making individual parts:

The full-size patterns are on p. 77.
See p. 79 for the full-size jacket motif.

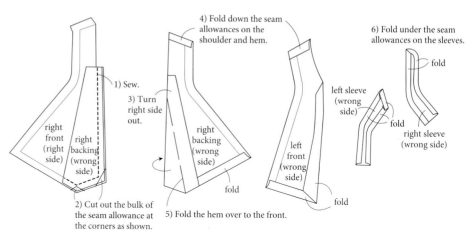

4) Fold down the seam allowances on the shoulder and hem.

6) Fold under the seam allowances on the sleeves.

1) Sew.

3) Turn right side out.

right front (right side)

right backing (wrong side)

right backing (wrong side)

left front (wrong side)

left sleeve (wrong side)

fold

right sleeve (wrong side)

fold

fold

fold

fold

2) Cut out the bulk of the seam allowance at the corners as shown.

5) Fold the hem over to the front.

2. Stitching individual parts to the background fabric:

1) Mark the lines (see the full-size pattern on p. 79) on the background fabric as a guide to sew on the coat.

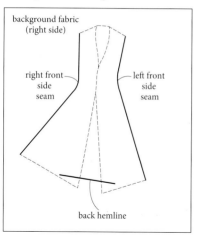

background fabric (right side)

right front side seam

left front side seam

back hemline

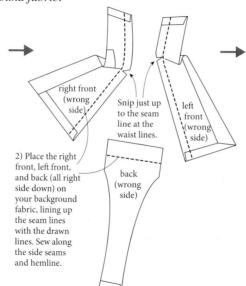

right front (wrong side)

Snip just up to the seam line at the waist lines.

left front (wrong side)

back (wrong side)

fold

2) Place the right front, left front, and back (all right side down) on your background fabric, lining up the seam lines with the drawn lines. Sew along the side seams and hemline.

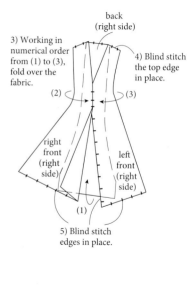

back (right side)

3) Working in numerical order from (1) to (3), fold over the fabric.

4) Blind stitch the top edge in place.

(2)

(3)

right front (right side)

left front (right side)

(1)

5) Blind stitch edges in place.

3. Adding the sleeves:

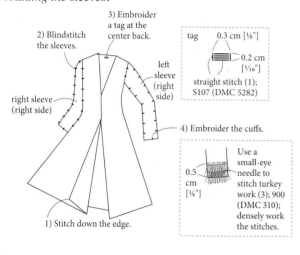

2) Blindstitch the sleeves.

3) Embroider a tag at the center back.

left sleeve (right side)

right sleeve (right side)

1) Stitch down the edge.

tag

0.3 cm [⅛"]

0.2 cm [1/16"]

straight stitch (1); S107 (DMC 5282)

4) Embroider the cuffs.

0.5 cm [¼"]

Use a small-eye needle to stitch turkey work (3); 900 (DMC 310); densely work the stitches.

4. Embroidering and adding the collar:

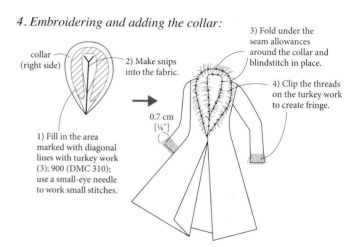

collar (right side)

2) Make snips into the fabric.

3) Fold under the seam allowances around the collar and blindstitch in place.

4) Clip the threads on the turkey work to create fringe.

0.7 cm [¼"]

1) Fill in the area marked with diagonal lines with turkey work (3); 900 (DMC 310); use a small-eye needle to work small stitches.

Bundle Up

shown on page 35

- The full-size Bundle Up embroidery patterns are below.
- The number in the parentheses stands for the number of strands used for the specific stitch.
- The Olympus embroidery floss number follows each stitch; because Olympus floss is not widely available outside Japan, we have included the DMC floss number in parentheses.

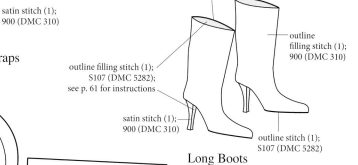

satin stitch (1);
486 (DMC 414)

for the thumb only,
double satin stitch (1);
486 (DMC 414)

direction of the double
satin stitch

turkey work (2);
900 (DMC 310)

Fur Gloves

split stitch (1);
900 (DMC 310);
work two rows to
fill in wide areas;
see p. 58 for instructions

Work satin stitches in
the shape of diamonds
to create a crosshatch
quilting pattern.

satin stitch (1);
900 (DMC 310)

lazy daisy stitch (1);
S105 (DMC 5283)

straight stitch (2);
900 (DMC 310)

satin stitch (1);
900 (DMC 310)

satin stitch (1);
900 (DMC 310)

Sunglasses

Bag with Chain Straps

outline stitch (1);
900 (DMC 310)

outline
filling stitch (1);
900 (DMC 310)

outline filling stitch (1);
S107 (DMC 5282);
see p. 61 for instructions

satin stitch (1);
900 (DMC 310)

outline stitch (1);
S107 (DMC 5282)

Long Boots

Full-size black coat pattern
Patterns include seam allowances.
Put the templates on the fabric and cut out pieces.

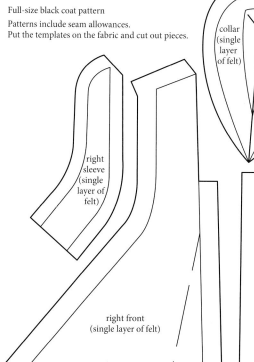

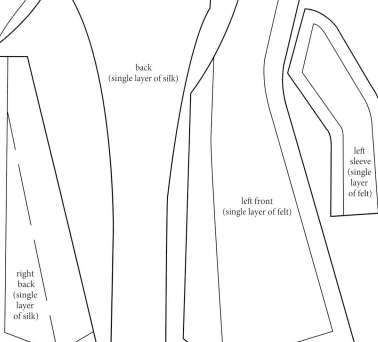

collar
(single
layer
of felt)

right
sleeve
(single
layer of
felt)

right front
(single layer of felt)

right
back
(single
layer
of silk)

back
(single layer of silk)

left front
(single layer of felt)

left
sleeve
(single
layer
of felt)

Sunglasses bag and Chandelier bag

shown on pages 36, 37

Materials needed

Linen (bag exterior), 60 x 40 cm (24" x 16")
Printed fabric (bag lining), 60 x 40 cm (24" x 16")
Interfacing, 90 x 80 cm (36" x 32")
Leather trim for handles, two 1.5 x 50 cm (⅝" x 19¾") pieces
Embroidery floss: black

1. Embroidering and cutting fabric pieces:

1) Using the measurements shown below, draw
lines on the fabric and cut out the fabric pieces.

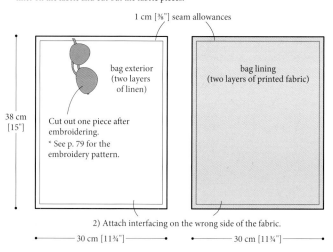

1 cm [⅜"] seam allowances

bag exterior
(two layers
of linen)

Cut out one piece after
embroidering.
* See p. 79 for the
embroidery pattern.

bag lining
(two layers of printed fabric)

38 cm
[15"]

2) Attach interfacing on the wrong side of the fabric.

30 cm [11¾"]   30 cm [11¾"]

2. Attaching the handles:

3. Assembling the bag:

4. Finishing the bag:

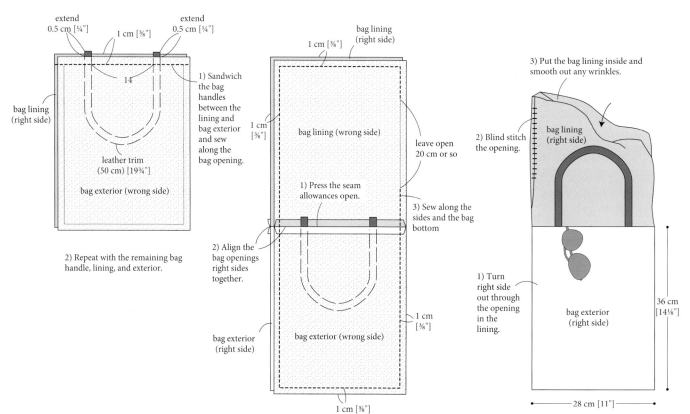

2. Attaching the handles:

extend
0.5 cm [¼"]   1 cm [⅜"]   extend
0.5 cm [¼"]

14

bag lining
(right side)

1) Sandwich
the bag
handles
between the
lining and
bag exterior
and sew
along the
bag opening.

leather trim
(50 cm) [19¾"]

bag exterior (wrong side)

2) Repeat with the remaining bag
handle, lining, and exterior.

3. Assembling the bag:

bag lining
(right side)

1 cm [⅜"]

1 cm
[⅜"]

bag lining (wrong side)

leave open
20 cm or so

1) Press the seam
allowances open.

3) Sew along the
sides and the bag
bottom

2) Align the
bag openings
right sides
together.

bag exterior
(right side)

bag exterior (wrong side)

1 cm
[⅜"]

1 cm [⅜"]

4. Finishing the bag:

3) Put the bag lining inside and
smooth out any wrinkles.

bag lining
(right side)

2) Blind stitch
the opening.

1) Turn
right side
out through
the opening
in the
lining.

bag exterior
(right side)

36 cm
[14⅛"]

28 cm [11"]

Sunglasses and Chandelier

shown on pages 36, 37

p. 37: Chandelier Bag

- The reduced Sunglasses embroidery pattern is below. Enlarge the pattern by 200% on a copier.
- The full-size Chandelier embroidery pattern is at right.
- See p. 61 for instructions on the outline filling stitch.
- The number in the parentheses stands for the number of strands used for the specific stitch.
- The Olympus embroidery floss number follows each stitch; because Olympus floss is not widely available outside Japan, we have included the DMC floss number in parentheses.

bag cutting line

bag seam line

Use color 900 (DMC 310) for all areas.
Fill in with satin stitches (1) for all areas
unless otherwise specified.

p. 36: Sunglasses bag

bag cutting line

bag seam line

satin stitch (2)

outline stitch (3)

satin stitch (2);
900 (DMC 310)

split stitch (1)
(see p. 58 for instructions)

outline filling stitch (2);
900 (DMC 310)

French knot stitch (2);
wrap two times

p. 34 Black coat

Mark lines on the
background fabric as a guide
to sew on the coat motif.

fly stitch (3)

right front
side seam

left front
side seam

outline
filling stitch (2);

Work a lazy daisy stitch (2) around a
French knot stitch (2); wrap two times.

lazy
daisy
stitch (2)

French knot
stitch (2);
wrap two times

back hemline

Reiko Mori

Born into a trading merchant family in Osaka, Reiko grew up having access to fabric and other materials from around the world. She spent her teen years immersing herself in handcrafts and fashion with her mother, who enjoyed sewing. She moved to Tokyo when she was 20 years old and began her career working for a magazine. She married, became a mother, and raised her growing family but had a dream of working with fabric. In 2000, she opened a shop featuring handmade goods called Love Letter in the Setagaya district of Tokyo. Around the same time she also became fascinated with computer software and the ability to work on 3D objects. This led her to begin designing embroidery patterns using 3D aspects.

Along with authoring books, she also teaches sewing and embroidery classes, which she considers to be an opportunity for her to learn. Her books in Japanese include *Embroidering on Linen, Simple Style, In Love with Embroidery* (published by Bunka Publishing Bureau), and *Reiko Mori's Flower Embroidery* (published by E & G Creates Co., Ltd.).

Love Letter
4-1-1 Kyodo, Setagaya-ku, Tokyo JAPAN
Tel: +81-(3)-3439-5892
http://www.loveletter2000.com

- -

Original Title	Elegant Embroidery: Embroidery Lessons from Reiko Mori
Author	©2015 Reiko Mori
First Edition	Originally published in Japan in 2015
Published by:	E & G Creates Co., Ltd.
	T's Loft 4F, 1-1-9, Nishikubo, Musashino-shi, Tokyo, 180-0013 JAPAN
	Tel: +81-(422)-55-5460
Translation	©2018 Stitch Publications, LLC
English Translation Rights	Arranged with Stitch Publications, LLC through Tuttle-Mori Agency, Inc.
Published by:	Stitch Publications, LLC
	Seattle, WA, USA
	http://www.stitchpublications.com
Distributed exclusively by:	Martingale®
	19021 120th Avenue NE, Ste. 102
	Bothell, WA 98011, USA
	http://www.martingale-pub.com
Printed & Bound	KHL Printing, Singapore
ISBN	978-0-9863029-5-4
PCN	Library of Congress Control Number: 2017958272

Production Megumi Tomiki, Junko Uchida, Teruko Iizuka, Akiko Kimura, Kazuko Mori, Mariko Imagawa, Etsuko Yoshimura, Naomi Kawate, Keiko Tatsuno

Staff
Book Design Mizuho Hayashi
Photography Yoshikatsu Watanabe (finished projects) Nobuhiko Honma (pages 38–43)
Pattern and Instructions Hiroko Higo
Illustrations Ikumi Shirai
Planning and Editing E & G Creates (Akiko Yabu), Hiroko Higo

- -

This English edition is published by arrangement with E & G Creates Co., Ltd. through Tuttle-Mori Agency, Inc.